HAVING IT
Y'ALL

HAVING IT Y'ALL

The Official Handbook for Citizens of the South
and Those Who Wish They Were

ANN BARRETT BATSON

RUTLEDGE HILL PRESS
Nashville, Tennessee

Published in Nashville, Tennessee, by Rutledge Hill Press,
211 Seventh Avenue North, Nashville, Tennessee 37219

Typography by D&T/Bailey Typography, Nashville, Tennessee
Art by Tonya Pitkin Presley, Studio III Productions
Southern Styles by Doug Montross

Library of Congress Cataloging-in-Publication Data

Batson, Ann Barrett, 1954–
    Having it y'all : the official handbook for citizens of the South
  and those who wish they were / Ann Barrett Batson.
       p. cm.
     ISBN 1-55853-234-X
     1. Southern States—Social life and customs—1865– I. Title.
  F215.2B393   1993
  975'.04—dc20   93-15829
                                                         CIP

Printed in the United States of America
    4 5 6 7 8—98 97

ACKNOWLEDGMENTS

Heartfelt thanks are due to the many folks, all paragons of Southern Style, who lent their advice, knowledge, and support during the arduous process of bringing *Having It Y'all* into the world. God bless you all (as we're fond of saying in Dixie), including:

Dale, Bill, and Brian Prentiss; Cindy Seibert; Pam Brown; Barry Landsman; Alan Ethridge; Katherine Koshewa; Helon Winn; Soo Peer; Sheila Murray; Malcolm Douglas; Nancy Wood; Allison Lucas; David Newell; Barbara Barrett; Elizabeth B. Barber; Sandy and Doug Mickle; Joy Dillingham; Dawn Carpenter; Mary Wis Estes; Ann Welch; Laura Anderson; Susan Storey; Val Kersey; Brenda Davis; Tim Seibert; Marvin Seibert; Mrs. James M. Hirs; Mrs. Tommy Praytor; James Levatino; Jocelyn and Frank McGuire; Deanna Conner; Renee Busby; Susan Fincher; Tara Prince.

Landsman Photography; the Country Music Association; the Association of Junior Leagues, Inc.; tourism and development boards of the states of Alabama, Arkansas, Georgia, Kentucky, Louisiana, Mississippi, North Carolina, South Carolina, Tennessee, and Virginia; Atlanta Public Library, Buckhead Branch; The Coca-Cola Company.

To my dear parents
_____

Elizabeth B. Batson
and
Hubert D. Batson
_____

with much love and gratitude

CONTENTS

Credits

HAVING IT
Y'ALL

CHAPTER ONE

Profiles in Southern Style

The Genuine Lowdown on the Southern State of Mind

It's a universal truth that Southerners are just downright different from everybody else. Also true is that we happen to be downright proud of this fact. Not that we mean to sound smug, but quite honestly, we do feel rather privileged. Let's face it: having your own world-famous culture is not something that folks from, say, Peoria or Katmandu can lay claim to.

Just what accounts for that certain mystique, that *je ne sais quoi*? What makes us Southerners and our homeland so treasured, so envied, and so misunderstood—often all at once? Well, more stuff than you could learn in a lifetime. There are plenty of scholars who have devoted their careers to making sense of the South and guess what? No one's nailed the definitive theory yet. (It's probably better that way. Some mysteries are sacred.)

Fortunately, you don't have to be a sociologist or historian to be on a first-name basis with the Southland. Heck, you don't even have to be smart; just turn the page and pay attention. This here's the official handbook for citizens and aficionados of the South . . . and those who wish they were.

THE SOUTHERN BIRTHRIGHT

Of all the millions of people in the world, only a relatively small number will have the divinely conferred destiny to be a born Southerner. And since life in the Southland is pretty darn close to heaven on earth, those of us who were blessed with this birthright quite naturally feel like the Chosen People. This explains why words such as *angst* and *ennui* have near-obscure status in the southern vocabulary and why, instead, we're inclined to wear a big grin and deliver such spontaneous proclamations as "I'm as happy as a pig in——," "Southern by the grace of God," or "Take me now, Jesus."

Being a divinely granted privilege, the Southern Birthright cannot be bought, sold, or transferred. You either have it or you don't. If you do, no doubt you thank the good Lord daily for your great fortune (or your predestination). If you don't, but wish you did, don't despair. Here's how to get yourself inducted in our ever-swelling ranks of happily naturalized Southerners:

1. First and foremost, set up a homestead in the Southland and learn firsthand about the southern way of life. Seeing may be believing, but to understand and enjoy it truly, you're going to have to go whole hog. That means nothing short of total immersion. So read on, then pack your bags.

2. Next, marry into a southern family. You will instantly and to overwhelming effect be grafted onto a family tree of unimaginably southern proportions. And even if the marriage doesn't last, you'll find all that Southernness has run rampant over you—like kudzu and just as everlasting.*

3. Later, permanently write yourself into southern genealogy by parenting a passel of southern young'uns. Your efforts will assure you perpetuity in the Dixie roll call, and your progeny will be the ordained beneficiaries of the ultimate gift of life: a Southern Birthright.

*Should your efforts fail at finding a spouse, fear not. Southern churches will welcome you with open arms and adopt you into their own sizable family.

SOUTHERNER'S CITIZENSHIP QUIZ

So you say you're a citizen of the South and proud of it? Then put your reputation where your mouth is with this Southerner's Citizenship Quiz. In five minutes you can prove whether you do indeed hail from the Southland or you're just whistlin' Dixie.

1. What is "The pod of the Gods"?
2. What Pray-TV evangelist and country music troubadours are cousins?
3. What was the name of Scarlett O'Hara's first husband?
4. Which southern state was the first to secede from the Union, and which was the first to be readmitted?
5. What is a "green front" store?
6. What is pot likker?
7. Who was the "First Family of Country Music"?
8. Which Southerner founded the Girl Scouts of America, and in which southern city did this occur?
9. Name the two winningest collegiate football coaches in history and the universities at which they claimed their records.
10. The world's first rock and roll star hailed from the Southland. What was his middle name?
11. What Dixie state is known as the undisputed "Catfish Capital of the World"?
12. Which southern baseball hero broke Babe Ruth's lifetime record for home runs, and for what team was he playing when he made history?
13. List the ingredients in a mint julep.

14. *Vidalia* refers to
    A) a speckled bird indigenous to the Carolina coast
    B) an onion revered for its sweet taste
    C) the site of a famous Civil War battle in Arkansas
15. Where did the world's first powered aircraft flight occur?
16. In which southern state was Walton's Mountain, of prime time television fame, situated?
17. What action did Rosa Parks take on behalf of the nascent civil rights movement in 1955?
18. For what literary contribution is Joel Chandler Harris best known?
19. To what insect did the town of Enterprise, Alabama, erect a monument, and why?
20. What famous general of the Confederate States of America was accidentally shot to death by one of his own troops?

(Answers on page 17)

Scoring:
8 or less correct answers: *Plumb Puny!* You must be a visitor.
9–14 correct answers: *Fair to Middlin'.* There's room for improvement.
15 or more correct answers: *Bodacious!* You know the South like the back of your hand.

KEYS TO THE SOUTHERN PSYCHE

The heart of every Southerner beats in steady three-quarter time to the universal rhythm of Southernhood. Not to sound corny, but each and every one of us moves in cultural unison for a reason—well, actually three: something best described as the holy trinity of the southern psyche. They're the radiant forces behind our singular identity and world view, the sources from whence all things southern cometh. They're the keys to entering the southern kingdom—or at least having a prayer of figuring it out.

■ KEY #1: We Have a Profound Sense of Place.

Eudora Welty, one of our famous authors, spoke with the voice of a true native daughter when she penned this phrase. We Southerners *do* have a proprietary sense of belonging and allegiance to our Southland and people. (We're special!) Steeped in the rural tradition, strengthened by a heritage of setbacks and hard-ups, and bound by a fierce love for God, family, and the land, this place is located in the collective heart and soul of all Southerners, wherever we may be.

■ KEY #2: We Live by Godly Precepts.

Our typically benevolent and unpretentious ways are deeply rooted in the God-fearing teachings of countless church sermons and Sunday school lessons. Oft-repeated prescripts such as "Thou shalt love thy neighbor as thyself," "Do unto others as you would have them do unto you," and the always-reliable "What would Jesus do?" helped spawn such admired southern social conventions as a kind word, a pleasant smile, and a good turn to friends and strangers alike.

■ KEY #3: We Live for Today and Have Faith In Tomorrow.

We've learned from experience to enjoy what we have while it's ours, because the only thing we know for sure is that nothing is for sure or forever (scholars are right fond of calling this the "southern sense of tragedy" and our preachers call it "God's will").

We also know from experience that if our somethings indeed become nothings, why it's a fact that you can't keep a good old boy or gal down for long. In the immortal words of Scarlett O'Hara: "I'll think of it all tomorrow. . . . I can stand it then. After all, tomorrow is another day." While scholars and shrinks like to call *this* "the South's heritage of denial," it's really the epitome of southern-style pragmatism at its best.

WHERE'S THE SOUTHLAND?

Down South. Deep South. Old South. New South. Would the real South please stand up?

As if our beloved Southland were not already filled with fascinating cultural conundrums, there's the ever-debated matter of determining just where to draw the line around all this sociology.

It doesn't help that we don't even officially exist—that point was conceded back last century—but let's not allow a mere technicality like that to get in the way. What's more liable to hang you up in your search for the Southland are just plain old bad directions. Rely on these counterfeit theories for drawing the line around Dixie and not only will you probably be bored to tears (you could be eating barbecue instead!), you'll be no closer to locating your destination:

1. *The Mason-Dixon Line:* Look away, look away, folks, because this is one confusing signpost. Take South Florida (please), which falls below the Line: need we say more? Consider Maryland, also below the Line, but whose ties to the South have gotten hard to spot—resulting in no small part from its proximity to the Northeast. And as for Texas? Well, they said it best: it's a whole other country.

2. *The War:* Yes, the War Between the States transformed a region into a nation—for a while, anyway. But Kentucky was a Confederate States of America holdout, while our southwestern cousins in Texas pledged allegiance. And by War's end, just about all the Confederate states could agree upon was that they'd had enough. All in all, there are better ways to define the Southland more than 130 years later.

3. *U.S. Government:* It may be official, but it's for sure that the U.S. government is no voice of authority on this subject so close to home. What Uncle Sam calls the South is an arbitrary catch-all of the sixteen states that just happen to be in the lower right-hand corner of the U.S. map (he was generous enough to toss in Washington, D.C., too). This alleged region may provide a convenient repository for statistics peculiar to the "South," but it will leave you clueless as to what, if any, connection it has with the genuine Southland.

The most reliable (fail-safe, in fact) way to get a fix on the real-and-sure-enough Southland doesn't even pretend to be so pseudo-cerebral. Like us, it's far more heartfelt. All you need to do? *Tune in for the telltale signs of Southern Style.* Plant yourself in a supposed vicinity of the Southland and look for the cultural markers that by the laws of God and nature make us what we are (something we'll have more to say about shortly). When you can spot those qualifying characteristics, you'll find your feet are standing on true southern soil. It's that simple, and that foolproof.

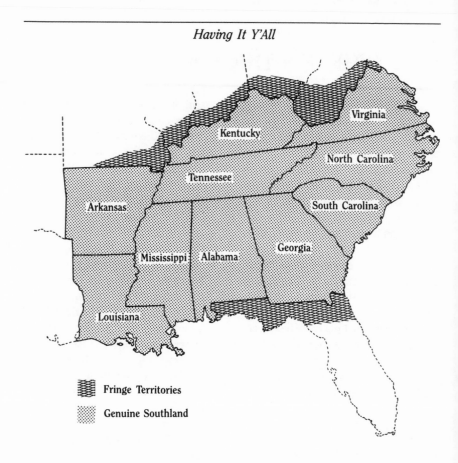

Fringe Territories

Genuine Southland

One favorite and dependable litmus test is to ask a presumed Southerner if he or she can direct you to a nearby restaurant or coffee shop (don't say "diner," a Yankee term) where you can get some grits and ham and red-eye gravy. If you're given fast affirmation, say grace and head for some good food: you're smack inside the provinces of the real South.

Applying this and other investigatory methods ourselves, we've come up with a conclusive map of the Southland, which follows. We suggest you take advantage of every opportunity to personally verify it. What better way to see what the South's all about?

■ **Which South did you have in mind? It all depends.**

Down South: Refers to our geographic location on a map of the United States and all that implies. Also a term of comparison and distinction; for instance, "People are just friendlier Down South." (Meaning: "You Yankees are stuck up and condescending, but I won't say that since it's not nice.")

Deep South: Describes lowermost, coastal southern states: Alabama, Mississippi, Louisiana, Georgia, South Carolina. Sometimes a euphemism for the Old South (see next). To non–Southerners, can be a pejorative term (as in, ugly, backwoods, prejudiced, dirt-eating).

Old South: The land of cotton, antebellum mansions, magnolias, and southern aristocracy. The place where the whole business of slavery became just that. Now the business of the Old South is the mansions and homes and a glamourous version of the pre-war days. (True Southerners will do what they must to assure the future of the homeplace—even open it to tourists.)

New South: The Southland of the twenty-first century. Home of the newest U.S. president and vice president, host to the 1996 Summer Olympics. Striving to show the world that we *can* be southern and worldly. (Only time will tell whether this proves to be our salvation or eventual extinction. Folks have their opinions.)

Answers to "Southerner's Citizenship Quiz" on page 13.

1. Okra. 2. Jimmie Lee Swaggart, Mickey Gilley, and Jerry Lee Lewis (all are first cousins). 3. Charles Hamilton. 4. South Carolina (December 20, 1860); Tennessee (July 24, 1866). 5. A state-owned and operated liquor store. 6. The broth formed by cooking beans, peas, or turnip greens with a hambone, which is usually ladled over these vegetables when served, then sopped up with cornbread. 7. The Carters (A. P., Sara, and Maybelle). 8. Juliette Gordon Low; in Savannah, Georgia. 9. Eddie Robinson, at Grambling State University; Paul ("Bear") Bryant, at the University of Alabama. 10. Elvis Aron Presley. 11. Mississippi. 12. Henry ("Hank the Hammer") Aaron, in 1974 while playing for the Atlanta Braves. 13. Sugar water, mint leaves, crushed ice, and bourbon whiskey. 14. B. 15. On Kill Devil Hill at Kitty Hawk, North Carolina. 16. Virginia. 17. She refused to relinquish her seat in the front of a Montgomery, Alabama, bus to a white man, thus sparking the beginning of an organized mass transit boycott by blacks and civil rights sympathizers. 18. His Uncle Remus stories (Uncle Remus: His Songs and His Sayings). 19. The boll weevil beetle. The insect's infestation and devastation of the region's cotton industry prompted the area to try peanut farming, which brought prosperity for the formerly destitute economy. 20. Thomas Jonathan ("Stonewall") Jackson.

THE TEN COMMANDMENTS OF SOUTHERN STYLE

True, the holy trinity of the southern psyche is what makes us tick, but just what makes Southerners so very, um, *southern?* Surely it's more than learning how to cook turnip greens or speaking with a "lazy" tongue (that's your terminology, not ours).

And you would be right: You can't just go out and crash-course your way into genuine Southernness. *Au contraire.* For all our visible singularities and peculiarities, you can't just act southern or get southern, you have to *be* southern. Being southern means you live in a relaxed state of grace, and such a station in life is not easy to obtain if you are not fortunate enough to have been born into it.

As a transplant, however, you can *evolve* to this pinnacle of existence. For as man evolved to the top of the food chain, so can lucky souls further evolve to true nirvana by faithfully practicing the Ten Commandments of Southern Style. Think of them as the way to heaven on earth. We do.

■ I. Thou Shalt Be a Friendly Folk.

Southerners just can't imagine going through life aloof and poker-faced. We were raised to behave in a sociable, neighborly fashion to our fellow man, even if we don't particularly like them or know them from a hole in the ground. First-time visitors to the South invariably receive our wholesale friendliness with astonishment, if not with guarded suspicion, but are soon eager to adopt our amicable ways for themselves.

If you've a hankering to do the same, rely on the following guidelines.

Being friendly to unknowns: Unless the strangers you encounter are most unsavory characters, behave as if you've known them since they were born. This means waving or smiling when passing (depending upon distance) and always greeting ("How you doin'?") if within earshot.

Being friendly to knowns: If the passerby is friend, family, or even mere acquaintance, the encounter should become a reunion of sorts. All participants should avidly discuss the weather, their health, and (always) any newly discovered tidbits of gossip or scandal. Always conclude the get-together with a fond farewell, such as "Now, you tell your sweet mama I said hello."

If the passerby is foe, smile especially kindly. Remember to turn the other cheek—at least in public.

■ II. Thou Shalt Maintain a Relaxed Lifestyle.

We Southerners are content to leave the frenetic way of life to people elsewhere. Even in big cities like Atlanta, we try our darnedest to keep things to a slow trot. Taking it easy is our form of preventive medicine and pop psychology. After all, since life is a journey, what's the use of not enjoying the ride?

Our respect for "quality of life" is hardly a new concept. We just never had a buzz word for it, until several of our towns and cities were "discovered" in rankings of the Best Places to Live (or Retire) in America. This would go a long way in explaining why many of the same detractors who used to deride us for living "in a time warp" or "so laid back they may as well be dead" are now moving Down South in droves. These folk are welcome to come on down and smell the magnolias if they'll keep one thing in mind: we don't care how you did it up North.

■ III. Thou Shalt Speak with a Drawl.

Just why do we Southerners loll our words around so? Not because we're lazy. Shucks, no. It's because they *taste* good. Being communicative sorts, we take our time when we talk so we can prolong the pleasure of the moment.

While one has to be raised Down South to "speak southern" authentically, it *is* possible for others to do a commendable job by keeping the fundamentals of southern speech in mind:

- Speak s-l-o-w-l-y. Savor the flavor of your words.
- Adopt a nasal twang and add a lilt to your tempo.
- Resist any inclination to enunciate precisely.
- Recognize that you must drop your jaw before your diphthongs can do likewise.
- End your sentences with a lift to your voice, as if you're asking a question.

- Incorporate the southern vernacular ("She's as cute as a speckled pup") into your everyday speech.
- Refer to chapter 3 for further tips.

■ IV. Thou Shalt Have Plenty to Say.

Like the mighty Mississippi, the oral tradition of the Southland runs deep and wide. In fact, it wouldn't be too much of an exaggeration to say that our vocal cords are connected to our hearts. This helps explain our long-standing and intensely emotional love affair with words spoken, sung, and written.

Outlets for our affection are easy to find. Just step into an evangelical church service for a firsthand encounter with sermonizing oratory or heavenward testifying. Ten minutes in the Piggly Wiggly grocery store or Singing River Mall offer plenty of chances to observe the gift of gab personified.

From gospel songfests to storytelling competitions, from our legislative chambers to our inimitable narrative literature, Southerners have such a proclivity for self-expression that the First Amendment could well be the most inalienable right of them all.

■ V. Thou Shalt All Be Related.

We Southerners not only belong to our homeland, we belong to one another. This is because the Southland is actually one massive extended family of relations and associations. Nearly every one of us can present some sort of connection, direct or distant, to almost anyone else from the Southland we have a mind to.

This means that if you are a Southerner, someone in a crowd will invariably know you, your mama, your daddy, your grandparents, and Lord knows who else in your family. Depending on your behavior, this fact of southern life can either give you a comfortable sense of belonging or make you uncomfortably paranoid.

It also means that everyone in town (and back home, too) knows about your current state of affairs, or will before the week is up, since Southerners are duty bound to follow up vigilantly on their brethren and inform everybody else about what they've learned.

Inherent in this social scrutiny is the comforting knowledge that no one goes alone in the Southland, because somebody always knows your business for better or worse. As a result, somebody's always there to help out at the drop of a hat. That's one of the best kinds of social security anybody could ever hope to have.

■ VI. Thou Shalt Show Good Manners.

Down South, we're justifiably famous for our gracious manners. Having good manners means being unfailingly polite, courteous, respectful, and helpful to relations, friends, and strangers. Having good manners qualifies one as "good folk," the designation of choice for all self-respecting Southerners.

Having bad manners means not exercising due diligence in the above and qualifies one for such nomenclature as "common," "rude," or (worst) "trash," all of which imply a fall from the good graces of the social order. Since only a thin line separates the Haves from the Have-Nots, those who are less than skilled in the protocol of good manners are urged to study carefully chapter 3.

■ VII. Thou Shalt Revel in Larrapin' Good Food.

If you think southern-style cooking is best exemplified by grits and greens, you've been watching too many "Beverly Hillbillies" reruns. Truth is, the mouths of the South delight in an enviable array of acclaimed cuisines which, though they may be home-grown, are definitely not just down-home.

That our ingenious forebears were passionate gastronomes is evidenced in such legendary southern cuisines as Creole and Cajun, Low Country coastal, Gulf Coast specialties, barbecue, country-style hams, burgoos and stews, and, of course, our honest-to-goodness home-style and soul-food cooking.

For a true view of this Southern Style incarnate, spend some time at the supper table. (chapter 6 will tide you over till mealtime.) It'll be a tribute to the bounty of our land, lakes, and seas, a shared celebration you'll not see the likes of outside the Southland.

■ VIII. Thou Shalt Possess a Touch of Country.

While the majority of Southerners now live outside of agraria, few of us will ever discard all the vestiges of our rural heritage, even should we be rash enough to try. You'd be hard pressed to find a Southerner who neither grew up in the country nor spent a childhood vacation with a country cousin, where more than a few hot afternoons were dedicated to picking and shelling snap beans, tending barnyard animals, or fishing in a pond.

The carry-over effects last a lifetime. Take a look, for example, at our penchant for pickup trucks. (Jeep Cherokees and Chevrolet Blazers are just citified variations on this theme.) Or at our innate hankering for fresh vegetables via backyard gardens, roadside vegetable trucks, farmers' markets, and home canning. And at our yearnings for lazy summer evenings on a front porch replete with rocking chairs, sofa swing, and the serenades of crickets and cicadas.

We could get even more long-winded and maybe a little misty-eyed about all this, but we think you get the message. There's a touch of country in us all Down South, and we figure it's one of the nicest touches to lay claim to.

■ IX. Thou Shalt Love the Lord Jesus.

Welcome to the Holyland Down South, a.k.a. the Bible Belt, Land of Pray-TV, the 10-percent tithe (that's gross income, mind you), and fundamentalist fervor. To millions of Southerners, religion is a subject that's taken *very* seriously. After all, eternal damnation is nothing to laugh about. So for folks of this persuasion, spreading the gospel goes on like there's no tomorrow since, according to the Holy Word, there may not be one.

With such almighty consequences at stake, it's not surprising that so many of our other-worldly brethren ceaselessly strive to promote the cause of the kingdom.

■ X. Thou Shalt Love the Southland.

Southerners are so unabashedly devoted to Dixie that the mere mention of the South prompts a warm feeling in our chests. The South is our homeland, our heritage, our collective identity. Small wonder, then, that so few of us have left the Southland behind for long and that most of us who have sojourned have also returned to the family fold like eager prodigal children.

It may sound trite to anyone who doesn't hail from here, but it's undeniably true: You can take a Southerner out of the South, but you'll *never* get the South out of the Southerner. Our land is in our blood, and it's always on our minds.

SOUTHERN STYLE #1: THE RAISED-RIGHTS
Brought up to be fine, upstanding citizens of the Southland.
("A good name is rather to be chosen than great riches.")

Wearing Polo cologne

Polo golf shirt

L. L. Bean
braided leather belt

Duckhead khakis
(pressed with hard crease)

Seiko watch
(Rolex Datejust clone with
Bulldog insignia)

Bass loafers

Pearl stud earrings

Citizen's gold watch
with mesh band

Dooney & Bourke
duo-tone leather
satchel

14k bangle bracelet

Talbot's dress

Unisa "skimmer" flats

HIM

Doug Marlette *HER*

Name: William Wirt Prentiss (goes by Bill)
Profession: Marketing Director, Medtech
  Corporation
Education: Myers Park High, Charlotte,
  NC, '74
BA, University of Georgia, '78
Drives: Ford Bronco II
Social Resume: Member of Hillcrest Methodist
  Church (Trustee since '84)
  Member suburban golf and swim club
  Active alumni, UGA
  Jaycees
  Coach, Little League team, '80, '81
  Ducks Unlimited
Book Last Read: The Firm, by John Grisham
Overheard saying: "How's your mama and
  them doin'?"

Name: Cathryn Ann (*nee* Watts) Roberts
Profession: Homemaker, supermom and
  former special ed teacher
Education: Dreher High, Columbia, SC, '74
B Ed, University of Georgia, '78
Drives: Buick Regal
Social Resume: Docent, Hedgepeth Oaks
  (antebellum mansion)
  Ways & Means Committee, annual Dogwood
  Festival
  Daisy Scouts troop leader
*Book Last Read: Fried Green Tomatoes at the
  Whistle Stop Cafe,* by Fannie Flagg
Overheard Saying: "Isn't that *precious*!?!"

PROFILES IN SOUTHERN STEREOTYPES

All right, let's get it over with: that mettlesome business of southern stereotypes—our cultural baggage, those thorns in our collective side, those caricatured ghosts of generations past that are constantly rebounded to us with a heavy topspin.

If you're a Southerner, you already know what we're talking about. You're more than familiar with the opinions of those smug representatives from more *fortunate* regions who can't *believe* somebody as nice as you would willingly live in such a *backward, impoverished* place among such *bizarre* characters. "Do you drink moonshine?" they want to know, and "Do you know anyone in the KKK?" Invariably we're asked, "Do you live on a plantation like Tara?" or (honestly, we're not making these up), "Do you have shopping centers down there?" Ask these self-professed cultural experts to describe a typical Southerner, and you can bet money you'll hear about the fabled caricatures below.

Now, we won't tell you that these overdrawn figures are total inventions. The point is that the reputation of these skeletons in our sociological closet looms exponentially larger than their population. The vast majority of us are pretty much just regular folk who live by the commandments of Southern Style.

■ **Stereotype #1: The Southern Aristocrats**

Baptized with a Jefferson cup and raised by colored mammies, the Southern Aristocrats know that—one day—the South will rise again. They while away languid hours at their Taraesque mansions, planning lawn parties and barbecues. She's as pale and fragile as bone china, as highstrung as a Kentucky racehorse, and an irrepressible flirt. He's a bourbon-swigging, cigar-smoking poker player who likes to bag quail, ducks, and women every chance he gets. For them, time is permanently suspended in a vignette of nineteenth-century provincialism predating the arrival of the Recent Unpleasantness.

■ **Stereotype #2: The White Supremacist**

He's got Red Man tobacco in his cheek, a Confederate flag in his fist, and white sheets in the closet. He knows that—one day—the South will surely rise again. This character's the unrepentant racist who has little respect for anyone who's not white, southern, and male. A heart of stone and a narrow mind are standard equipment on this model, whose mission in life is to restore the South to the former glory days of the old order and whose idea of a joy ride entails firebombs, threats, and other similar recreation.

■ Stereotype #3: The Fanatic Fundamentalists

They're the flash and brash of the Bible Belt, and they know that—one day soon—Jesus will come again. In anticipation of that out-of-this-world event, all the tent's a stage of hellfire-and-brimstone sermonizing, holy rolling and prophesying, faith healing, and snake handling. Every street corner's a pulpit for delivering stoked-up, Bible-thumping invocations and exhortations ("Get right with God!" "Repent and be saved!"); every passerby's a recruit to be plucked from the clutches of Satan. And because the end is near, there's never an end to this heavenly action on earth.

THE SOUTH ACCORDING TO HOLLYWOOD

When it comes to cinematic portrayals, the South and Southerners invariably fall prey to the same old clichés as cowboys and Indians or cops and robbers—heavy on the hyperbole, light on the variety, and short on substance. Now this may be entertainment (of a sort), but it ain't the South we know and love.

Recognize these?

■ The Antebellum South

The cinematic version of the Southern Aristocrat. Often an epic tragedy, the orderly and halcyon life of southern landed gentry is felled at the hands of Yankees. You can count on women to be presented as either coquettish southern belles or saintly southern ladies, men as hot-headed but weak-willed idealists, and blacks as loyal, obedient slaves. Most familiar examples: *Gone With the Wind; Shenandoah.*

■ The Fallen South (a.k.a. Southern Gothic)

Melancholy moral tales about the decay and collapse of the southern social order. Eccentric and flamboyant characters despair their circumstances but are unable to accept change. Most familiar examples: *The Long, Hot Summer; A Streetcar Named Desire; Jezebel; Wise Blood.*

■ The Backwoods South

Spoofs of southern country bumpkins crossing paths with city folk. A big fixture on prime time television during the 1960s and, to this day, on syndicated reruns. Most familiar examples: *The Weavers;* "The Beverly Hillbillies"; "Green Acres."

■ The Good Ole Boy South

Modern-day Johnny Rebs race cars, chase women, and plot to outsmart dumb, pot-bellied state troopers. Waylon and Willie, chewing tobacco, six-packs, and sassy good old girls are ever-present fixtures in this genre. Most-familiar examples: *Smokey and the Bandit (I, II, III); Macon County Line; Cannonball Express;* "Dukes of Hazzard."

■ The Evil South

Racist, redneck monsters have for lunch anyone who has the bad luck to cross their paths. Most familiar examples: *Deliverance; Easy Rider; In the Heat of the Night* (movie); *Mississippi Burning.*

CHAPTER TWO

A Look Back

How We've Made History
and What We Have to Show for It

Even before Charles Mason and Jeremiah Dixon were knee-high to a surveyor's level, there was history aplenty being made down this way. We've never let up, nor do we plan to.

Where else but the Southland could such all-American institutions as bourbon whiskey, Coca-Cola, and the Moon Pie have been inspired? Who else but Southerners would have the spunk to insist, "Give me liberty or give me death!" and, nearly 200 years later, "I have a dream!"? And from where else but the South could both the father of our country and the king of rock and roll hail? The answers are, of course, nowhere, nobody, and nowhere.

The same goes for many more of our claims to fame (and our fair share of claims to shame)—so many, in fact, that we'll just let history speak for itself.

SOUTHLAND TIMELINE

A March Through Southern History

■ **Before the War: The first of the South's three historical epochs.**

1607: First permanent English settlement in America is established at Jamestown colony, Virginia.

1693: Academia arrives in the South with establishment of Virginia's William and Mary College.

1755: Acadians are expelled from Canada; they later migrate to Louisiana territory to build Cajun communities.

1775: Virginian Patrick Henry declares, "Give me liberty or give me death."

1776: First U.S. scholastic fraternity, Phi Beta Kappa, is founded at Virginia's William and Mary College.

1776: Congress adopts Declaration of Independence, drafted by Virginia planter Thomas Jefferson.

Eli Whitney

1792: Yankee Eli Whitney invents cotton gin while in Georgia; he helps cotton become king in South.

1795: America's first state university is founded in Chapel Hill, North Carolina.

1801: Virginia planter Thomas Jefferson is inaugurated third president of the United States.

1803: France cedes Louisiana Territory to United States for $15 million.

1814: General Andrew Jackson defeats Creek Indians at battle of Horseshoe Bend.

1828: U.S. Congress passes "Tariff of Abominations"; South Carolina's protest begins sectionalism in South.

1828: Nation's first gold rush begins near Dahlonega, Georgia.

Patrick Henry

Davy Crockett at the battle of the Alamo

1829: Tennessee statesman Andrew Jackson is inaugurated seventh U.S. president: South Carolinian John C. Calhoun enters second term as vice president.

1830: First parade by a mystic society is held in Mobile, Alabama: America's Mardi Gras tradition is born.

1831: Black preacher Nat Turner leads bloodiest slave insurrection in southern history.

1831: Virginian Cyrus McCormick invents reaper and revolutionizes grain harvesting.

1835: James Crow of Kentucky, perfecter of sour mash bourbon distilling method, gives world his namesake whiskey.

1836: Tennessee frontiersman and politician Davy Crockett dies in battle at the Texas Alamo.

1842: Dr. Crawford Long of Georgia is first to use general anesthesia for humans.

1844: James K. Polk of Tennessee defeats Kentuckian Henry Clay for U.S. presidency.

1850: Henry Clay proposes Compromise of 1850 in Congress to mediate the growing North-South slavery disputes.

1857: U.S. Supreme Court denies Missouri slave Dred Scott his freedom; the controversy builds.

1859: Abolitionist John Brown hanged for insurgent efforts to liberate slaves.

■ **The War Between the States:
Southern Epoch #2.**

December 1860: South Carolina unanimously adopts Ordinance of Secession from United States; ten other southern states soon follow.

February 1861: The Confederate States of America convenes in Montgomery; Jefferson Davis is elected president.

April 1861: The War Between the States begins as Confederate guns fire on Fort Sumter, South Carolina.

May 1861: Confederate Congress declares war on United States.

March 1862: First ironclad battle ends underwater as C.S.S. *Virginia* and U.S.S. *Monitor* are sunk at Hampton Roads, Virginia.

September 1862: Key Confederate offensive at Antietam Creek, Maryland, is thwarted by Union troops; 23,000 casualties.

January 1863: President Abraham Lincoln issues Emancipation Proclamation, proclaiming freedom for all slaves.

July 1863: Confederate army suffers decisive defeat at Gettysburg, Pennsylvania.

July 1863: Vicksburg falls to Union forces; control of Mississippi River follows.

May 1864: U.S. General William T. Sherman starts rapacious march to the sea through Georgia.

August 1864: Admiral David Farragut urges, "Damn the torpedoes, full speed ahead," during his attack on Mobile Bay.

April 1865: General Robert E. Lee surrenders to General Ulysses S. Grant at Appomattox Court House, Virginia; the War Between the States officially ends.

The Virginia

WHY WE LOST THE CAUSE

You can read about this subject till the cows come home, but after all is said and done, the defeat of the Confederacy boils down to six fundamental issues:

1. Since the preservation of slavery was essential only to a very small but very wealthy and powerful group of Southerners, most who fought the War were defending a cause that had very little, if any, effect on their livelihood. The honor of this ideal eventually paled for many Confederate soldiers in the face of death and destruction. By the War's end, almost one-third of the Confederacy's troops had deserted their duty.

2. "There was more of them than there was of us." The Confederacy's population numbered about eleven million, contrasted with twenty-two million northerners and non-aligneds. Additionally, slaves made up nearly one-third of our nation, making it pretty clear that we were outnumbered from the moment we commenced the conflict.

3. We initiated the War with plenty of zeal but were nigh empty handed of such assets as an operational government, organized militia, a financial system, an industrial base, foreign trade rela-

tions, and, well, you get the gist.

4. Ironically, the pragmatic necessity of a sovereign government was handicapped by the South's own doctrine of state's rights. As a result, many efforts to build a more effective Confederate government were vetoed for the sake of separatism.

5. The primarily defensive military strategy of the Confederacy became its nemesis. War tacticians theorized that the North could be repelled repeatedly enough so that eventually it would abandon its attacks and that England and France would support the Confederacy to maintain the import trade from the Southland. However, neither theory panned out, and the North's offensive strategy to geographically divide and conquer the South proved successful.

6. Being a religious folk and believing in predestination, many Southerners came to interpret the Confederacy's inability to defeat the Union as God's will. Finding it increasingly difficult to justify the staggering loss of life and land in the name of slavery, a humbled Southland finally confessed its errancy and surrendered the Cause forever.

LEADERS AND HEROES OF THE CONFEDERACY

They're the legends of a past long gone, the icons of abandoned ideals. They nobly served their nation and gallantly defended a cause. Those standing tallest in this historical drama include:

■ General Robert Edward Lee

Commander-in-chief of the Confederate army. Although he personally abhorred secession and was offered field command of the Union army, Lee chose to defend the honor of his homeland. It was Lee who surrendered the Confederacy to Ulysses S. Grant at Appomattox Court House, ending the War. He later became the patriarch of Washington and Lee University.

Thomas J. ("Stonewall") Jackson

Robert E. Lee

■ Thomas Jonathan ("Stonewall") Jackson

One of the Confederacy's most brilliant tacticians. Stonewall Jackson led several key defensive Confederate campaigns; at the battle of Manassas, he earned his nickname after his troops unyieldingly held their line "like a stone wall." Tragically, in the confusion of battle at Chancellorsville, he was shot in the left arm by a Confederate soldier and died a week later.

■ Jefferson Davis

President of the Confederate States of America and former U.S. senator and U.S. secretary of war. Faced with the ultimately impossible task of building

Jefferson Davis

■ Lieutenant General Wade Hampton

South Carolinian chief of cavalry for the Confederacy. He prevented President Jeff Davis's capture at War's end and became governor of his home state.

■ Major General J.E.B Stuart

Virginia military officer whose clever leadership forged victories at Manassas and Chancellorsville. As commander of the Confederate cavalry at Gettysburg, his failure to support Lee's infantry sealed the fate of the Confederacy.

a nation from a cause, Davis strove to organize and equip the Confederacy for self-sufficiency. Imprisoned for two years after the War and denied his U.S. citizenship, he "carried the sins" of his people as the figurehead of the fallen Confederacy.

■ General P.G.T. Beauregard

Louisiana's legendary military hero, most admired for directing the assault on Fort Sumter, marshaling the victory at Manassas, and defending Charleston and Richmond.

■ Major General Nathan Bedford Forrest

Tennessee's expert military tactician who often resoundingly defeated or repelled Union attacks.

J. E. B. Stuart

Villains of the Lost Cause

■ Union General William Tecumseh Sherman

Sherman is indisputably the scoundrel primo and damnedest Yankee of them all. After reducing Atlanta to ashes in the fall of 1864, he engineered wholesale devastation with his march through Georgia to the sea (thoughtfully, however, he spared Savannah, presenting the lovely old city to Lincoln as a Christmas gift). Understandably, Sherman's name is still despised in many parts of Georgia, and nowhere in the Southland is it likely to arouse a gracious reception.

Ulysses S. Grant

William Tecumseh Sherman

■ Ulysses S. Grant

Supreme commander of the Union army. Grant was the mastermind of the Union campaigns that ultimately forced the surrender of the Confederacy. His tenure as president further ensured his villainous stature in the South; Reconstruction and his corrupt administration further worsened the postwar Southland's dire straits.

■ Yankee Carpetbaggers and Southern Scalawags

Opportunistic parasites who capitalized upon war-torn Dixie's reduced circumstances; viewed Down South as some of the most despicable, contemptible, and downright lowdown excuses for humanity in history. Not surprisingly, this opinion has changed very little over the last hundred years.

WAR NOMENCLATURE

■ What to Call the War

Southern culture dictates the use of historically and socially correct nomenclature to refer to the Blue-Gray conflict. Southerners who have been raised right will employ any of the following:

The War Between the States
The War of the Rebellion
The War for Southern Independence
The War of Secession
The War
The Lost Cause
The Late Unpleasantness
The Recent Altercation

■ What NOT to Call the War.

There is no better way to validate your citizenship (or your upbringing) than to avoid the erroneous term *Civil War* when referring to the War. Those who know better know there's a big difference.

Historians will tell you that the whole ruckus came about because many southern states wanted sovereignty, freedom to run their own affairs without outside interference. Their goal denied, eleven southern states seceded and fought for independence as the Confederate States of America, *not* to overthrow the U.S. government. To many Southerners the distinction between the two is enormous, which explains why some Dixie citizens still raise an eyebrow when they hear the War Between the States called the Civil War.

WAR TRIVIA

• The South's first major offensive effort, which occurred in 1862 at Sharpsburg, was likely lost due to the carelessness of a Confederate soldier. An observant Union soldier found three cigars, either dropped or discarded, wrapped in a CSA order. The information enabled Union General George B. McClellan to successfully repel Lee's army.

• The first Civil War monument was erected late in 1863 at the Shiloh battleground in southwestern Tennessee.

• More than $2 billion worth of Confederate currency was distributed during the War Between the States. As well, there were countless issues by states, counties, cities, railroads, and businesses, plus plenty of counterfeits. When the Confederate "blue backs" were first issued in 1861, they were valued at ninety-five cents on the U.S. dollar. By the War's end at Appomattox, their value was about one and one-half cents to the dollar.

• At the battle of Spotsylvania, Robert E. Lee's beloved horse, Traveller, became uncharacteristically frightened by a bursting shell and reared just in time for a cannonball to pass harmlessly under his girth. Traveller is now memorialized on the campus of Washington and Lee University in Virginia.

• Confederate General Nathan Bedford Forrest had twenty-nine horses shot from under him during the war.

• The "Rebel yell" is believed to have been used for the first time in the battle at First Bull Run (First Manassas) on July 21, 1861.

• Mary Todd Lincoln's brother was a Confederate surgeon, and each of her three sisters was married to a Confederate officer.

• Vicksburg, Mississippi, held out against Federal forces until General U. S. Grant held it under siege for six weeks in early summer 1863.

■ After the War: Southern Epoch #3

1865: Slavery is declared illegal with ratification of Thirteenth Amendment.

1867: Ku Klux Klan ("the Invisible Empire") is exposed in Tennessee newspaper story.

1868: Reconstruction begins with readmission of most southern states to Union. Carpetbaggers and scalawags emerge.

1868: Edmund McIlhenny of Louisiana first bottles Tabasco Sauce.

1873: Tennesseans Randolf McCoy and Floyd Hatfield squabble over hog stealing; family feud escalates across Tennessee, Kentucky, and West Virginia.

1875: First Kentucky Derby is held at Churchill Downs, for $2,850 purse.

1877: Carpetbag governments flee north with final removal of Federal troops.

1878: Most extensive yellow fever epidemic in nation's history ravages the Gulf states and Mississippi valley.

1881: Tuskegee Institute, vocational school for blacks, is chartered in Alabama under tutelage of Booker T. Washington.

1881: Br'er Rabbit and Tar Baby are introduced to America by Georgian Joel Chandler Harris in *Uncle Remus.*

1886: Henry Grady, Atlanta journalist, makes "New South" appeal to New York financiers.

1886: Atlanta pharmacist J. S. Pemberton concocts "delicious and refreshing" potion, calling it Coca-Cola.

1892: Tennessee salesman Joel O. Cheek's ready-to-perk coffee blend is a hit at Nashville's Maxwell House hotel.

Early members of the Ku Klux Klan

1894: United Daughters of the Confederacy is founded in Nashville, Tennessee.

1896: Southern agriculture is revitalized by George Washington Carver, who finds new uses for sweet potatoes, soybeans, and peanuts while at Tuskegee Institute.

1897: The Father of Country Music, Jimmie Rodgers, is born in Meridian, Mississippi.

1897: Jazz comes of age in New Orleans's Storyville district.

1900: Casey Jones dies at the throttle of the Cannon Ball Express in Mississippi; he's later immortalized in a popular ballad.

1901: Booker T. Washington's *Up from Slavery* is published; it becomes a best seller.

1903: Orville and Wilbur Wright make history in North Carolina with first flight of a heavier-than-air machine.

"The Grand Ole Opry" in full swing

1907: William H. Smith of Mississippi organizes the "Corn Club," precursor of 4-H Clubs of America.

1909: William Du Bois helps found National Association for the Advancement of Colored People during his tenure at Atlanta University.

1911: Alabamian and jazz great W. C. Handy composes "Memphis Blues."

1912: Juliette Gordon Low founds American Girl Scouts in Savannah, Georgia.

1913: Virginian Woodrow Wilson is inaugurated twenty-eighth U.S. president.

1913: North Carolinian Phillip Lance cooks up a snack food dynasty by selling roasted peanuts for five cents a bag.

1919: First Moon Pie is made by a Chattanooga bakery.

1919: Candler family sells Coca-Cola Company to Robert Woodruff for $25 million.

1919: Alabama town of Enterprise honors boll weevil by erecting first monument to an insect in United States.

1923: "The Grand Ole Opry" begins broadcasting from WSM in Nashville, Tennessee; it becomes longest-running continuously aired radio show in America.

1925: Tennessee schoolteacher John Scopes is convicted in "monkey trial" for teaching concepts of evolution.

1926: Virginian Richard Byrd is first to fly to North Pole and back.

1927: Almost 700,000 are homeless after worst Mississippi River flood in history.

1929: Delta Air Lines of Georgia begins passenger service and starts steady ascent to success.

1930: Kentuckian Robert Penn Warren's statement of southern agrarian ideals, *I'll Take My Stand,* is published.

1934: First Masters Golf Tournament is held at Augusta National Golf Club, Georgia.

1934: Notorious bank robbers Clyde Barrow and Bonnie Parker bite the dust in Louisiana.

1935: Senator Huey P. Long of Louisiana is assassinated.

Margaret Mitchell

"Kingfish" Huey P. Long

1935: Rural South is electrified by REA.

1936: Atlantan Margaret Mitchell's *Gone With the Wind* is published; sales top one million by year's end, and Pulitzer Prize follows.

1939: The movie *Gone With the Wind* opens at Loew's Grand in Atlanta.

1946: Kentucky's Duncan Hines helps pioneer cake mixes.

1947: Mississippi dramatist Tennessee Williams receives Pulitzer Prize for *A Streetcar Named Desire.*

1953: Hank Williams, King of

Country Music and Alabama native, dies.

1954: U.S. Supreme Court rules racial segregation in public schools violates Fourteenth Amendment, in *Brown* v. *Topeka Board of Education.*

1954: Son of Mississippi Elvis Presley records first hit, "That's All Right."

1954: Meteorite strikes woman in Sylacauga, Alabama.

1955: Rosa Parks is arrested for refusing to relinquish her seat on a Montgomery, Alabama, bus to a white man.

1956: "Colonel" Harlan Sanders makes fast food finger lickin' good with his Kentucky Fried Chicken.

1957: Nine black students attend Little Rock's Central High School under protection of Arkansas National Guard.

1960: U.S. manned space flight program takes off at Marshall Space Flight Center, Huntsville, Alabama.

1963: Martin Luther King, Jr., writes history with "I Have a Dream" speech on steps of Lincoln Memorial.

1965: More than 25,000 civil rights

supporters march from Selma to Montgomery to protest voter discrimination.

1966: Foxfire project debuts in Georgia: it documents the lives and customs of Southerners in Appalachia.

Dr. Martin Luther King, Jr.

1968: Martin Luther King, Jr., is assassinated in Memphis.

1969: Hurricane Camille wreaks havoc on Mississippi coast; 150 die.

1970: Ted Turner starts his superstation television dynasty.

1971: U.S. Supreme Court rules in favor of busing to achieve desegregation.

1972: Alabama politico George Wallace is paralyzed by assassin's bullet during his second campaign for president.

1973: Charles Hickson and Calvin Parker of Mississippi claim to be examined by aliens in a cigar-shaped spaceship.

1973: Tennessean Frederick Smith's expeditious Federal Express opens for business.

1974: Alabamian and Atlanta Brave Hank Aaron breaks Babe Ruth's home run record.

1976: Plains, Georgia, peanut farmer Jimmy Carter, Jr., is elected thirty-ninth president of the United States.

1977: The King of Rock and Roll, Elvis Presley, dies at age forty-two.

1977: Courageous Ted Turner wins America's Cup race.

1977: Georgian Bert Lance resigns from Jimmy Carter's cabinet amid accusations of monkey business in banking.

1979: Coca-Cola magnate Robert Woodruff makes history with $105

The South's populist president Jimmy Carter and his wife Rosalyn

40

million endowment to Emory University.

1980: President's brother, Billy Carter, is investigated by U.S. Senate for possible political ties with Libya.

1982: Knoxville, Tennessee, hosts World's Fair; most of the world stays home.

1984: New Orleans gives a World's Fair a try; it's another financial misfire for Dixie.

May 1985: New Coke is presented to America amidst great fanfare.

July 1985: New Coke goes flat; Coke "Classic" revived.

1986: Pro-academics prof and whistleblower Jan Kemp wins suit against University of Georgia's "athletics first" practices; gets $1.1 million.

1987: Holy wars of television evangelism commence when Jim and Tammy Bakker admit their unholy indulgences.

1989: Hurricane Hugo makes a direct hit on Charleston, South Carolina; devastation is staggering.

1989: Former PTL guru Jim Bakker is convicted of $158 million in unholy fraud and conspiracy.

1989: L. Douglas Wilder of Virginia becomes nation's first black governor.

1991: Former Klansman David Duke loses runoff election for governor of Louisiana; nation breathes sigh of relief.

1992: Arkansas Governor Bill Clinton and Tennessee Senator Albert Gore, Jr., are elected president and vice president of U.S.

1993: A young Elvis Presley is immortalized on a postage stamp chosen by public vote.

SOUTHERN STYLE #2:
POWER BROKERS OF THE NEW SOUTH
Proof positive that the traditional bastions of power-mongering Down South are crumbling like day-old biscuits.

Malcolm Greer Morgan
U.S. House of Representatives (R)
He's dancing as fast as he can around today's minefields of political correctness.

Tula Burroughs-Wiggins
City Councilwoman
They told her you can't fight city hall, but her social agenda is giving it a good shaking up.

Kathleen H. Kessler
Judge, U.S. Circuit Court
She's making mud pie out of the old boys' club—in a genteel manner, of course.

Rev. Samuel Grady Chandler, Jr.
Board of Directors, Southern Christian Leadership Conference; Senior Pastor, Zion AME Church
His faith can move mountains. So can just one of his phone calls.

TRIBUTES TO THE OLD SOUTH

Many Southerners periodically take time out to commemorate the Old South, making honorable mention of an epic chapter in our history and proudly admiring treasured artifacts of our antebellum heritage. While the Old South you'll encounter today is a once-removed relative of the original article, what endures are sterling heirlooms of early Southern Style, as these rituals will attest.

▪ Pilgrimages

A return to the Old South in the truest sense of the word, each spring the landmarks of antebellum prosperity are opened for a circuit of open houses. Known in some part of Dixie as "pilgrimages," the heartlands of pre-War staple-farming (cotton, sugar cane, and so forth) showcase their legacies with an annual tour week.

Grand flourishes of Southern Gothic preserved, the Deep South's pilgrimages make a conventional open house look like child's play. Awesome examples of the Greek Revival and Italianate styles (post-War homes excluded, thank you), situated on stately lawns and impressively furnished, draw disciples from all corners of the world to pay homage. Ladies in pre-War finery (often descendants of old Southern families) conduct the tours of these Deep South treasures with a mother's pride, an archivist's knowledge, and a commandant's authority.

Everybody takes it all *very* seriously. See for yourself, every March and April (contact each organization for details).

Mississippi

Natchez (also October): The grand dame of pilgrimages reveals the splendor of one of America's formerly wealthiest cities with thirty examples of antebellum splendor. Don't miss the Confederate pageant (topped off with a coronation of its annual king and queen) and other theatrical tributes to the Old South, The Pilgrimage is repeated in the fall. Contact: Natchez Pilgrimage Tour Association, P.O. Box 347, Natchez, 39120; 800/647-6742.

Columbus: Never attacked by Union forces, this city opens fifteen of its more than 100 impressive antebellum homes for two weekends. Contact: Columbus Convention and Visitors Bureau at 800/327-2686.

Vicksburg: Nine homes are included in the pilgrimage of this once thriving port and site of one of the Civil War's most important sieges. Contact: Vicksburg Convention and Visitors Bureau, P.O. Box 110, Vicksburg, 39180; 800/221-3536.

Port Gibson: The town that General Grant reputedly declared "too beautiful to burn" opens eight historic homes for its annual weekend pilgrimage. Contact: Port Gibson–Claiborne County Chamber of Commerce, P.O. Box 491, Port Gibson, 39150.

Alabama

Eufaula: Rivals Natchez in magnificence of antebellum heritage; more than ninety structures in this former river town are listed in the National Register of Historic Places. Contact: Eufaula Heritage Association, P.O. Box 486, Eufaula, 36027.

Selma: Visit antebellum homes dating from Selma's days as a flourishing riverboat and railroad center. Contact: Selma and Dallas County Chamber of Commerce, P.O. Drawer D, Selma, 36702.

Mobile: Amidst blooming azaleas, tour an array of nineteenth-century Federal-style townhouses, Creole cottages, and plantation homes. Contact: Historic Mobile Homes Tours, Inc., P.O. Box 66247, Mobile, 36660.

Georgia

Madison (also December): Spared Sherman's torch during his march through Georgia, twice a year Madison welcomes guests to many of its beautifully preserved antebellum homes. Contact: Madison Tours, Box 571, Madison, 30650.

Savannah: Walking tours of this port city's Federal-style homes and Greek Revival mansions have been a favorite spring ritual for more than fifty years. Contact: Savannah Tour of Homes & Gardens, 18 Abercorn Street, Savannah, 31401.

Louisiana

St. Francisville: Relive an early chapter in antebellum architectural history by visiting some of Louisiana's loveliest "cottage" style plantations during the annual Audubon Pilgrimage. Contact: West Feliciana Historical Society, Box 338, St. Francisville, 70775.

South Carolina

Charleston (also October): Twice-yearly walking tours in one of America's oldest cities showcase admirable examples of Adams-style and Greek Revival architecture. Contact: Festival of Houses, 51 Meeting Street, Charleston, 29401 (spring tours); The Preservation Society, 147 King Street, Charleston, 29401 (fall tours).

Georgetown: Elegant river plantations and historic city town homes attest to the antebellum bounty of indigo and rice. Annual plantation tours are a forty-year tradition here. Contact: Annual Plantation Tours, Prince George Winyah Parish, 300 Broad Street, Georgetown, 29440.

Beaufort (also October): In a town settled more than 400 years ago, striking examples of pre-Revolutionary and antebellum style architecture are featured in its Candlelight Tour. Contact; Historic Beaufort Foundation, P.O. Box 11, Beaufort, 29901.

■ The Lost Cause Remembered

Should you believe that the War holds fascination primarily for historians and senior citizens, you must have just fallen off the back of the turnip truck. Plenty of Southerners are avid students of the Lost Cause, and to some of them the saga of the Confederate States of America is akin to a Greek tragedy. Reminders of the Recent Altercation are abundant (there are *thousands* of war markers and memorials across Dixie), and often they're as large as life itself:

Re-enactments: The hue and cry of battle breaks forth on spring and fall weekends across the South, when encampments and re-enactments of the War Between the States are staged on historic battlefield sites. Replete with period uniforms (some descendants even sport family heirlooms) and antique munitions, re-enactments are the manly version of pilgrimages.

In May, more than 1,000 Blue and Gray soldiers converge upon Virginia Military Institute for ceremonial tribute to the battle of New Market in the Shenandoah Valley. In October, 500 participants re-enact Kentucky's most decisive battle at Perryville Battlefield State Shrine.

Artifacts Fairs: Those with a hankering for military memorabilia from the War Between the States can experience hog heaven several times a year at commemorative military shows and artifacts fairs. Enthusiasts and scholars alike will find a bonanza

Re-enactment scene

of uniforms, equipment, paintings, books, and other relics for sale or trade.

Between fairs, dyed-in-the-wool collectors can be found combing battlefield trenches for artifacts of war or paging through the latest issue of *Blue and Gray.*

Social Aspects: Don't fret if your ancestors didn't come over on the *Mayflower* or fight in the Revolutionary War. You're in Dixie, remember? If your forebears fought for the Confederate States of America, you've automatically qualified for a far more noble distinction. You can stake your place in the social register with membership in one of three stalwart salutes to the Lost Cause: *United Daughters of the Confederacy* (28,000 members), *Sons of Confederate Veterans* (12,500 members), or the more venerable *Military Order of the Stars and Bars,* for Sons of Confederate Veterans members whose ancestors served as commissioned officers (1,270 members).

Should you belong to these organizations, you're entitled to participate in activities ranging from the genteel (annual conventions and benevolent efforts) to the more controversial (such as the Daughters' successful block of North Carolina's 1979 decision to cease raising the Confederate flag on Confederate Memorial Day).

College-bound young southern gentlemen can pledge lifetime allegiance to the Old South through membership in *Kappa Alpha fraternity.* Founded at Washington and Lee University shortly after the War, Kappa Alpha brothers are sworn to emulate the integrity of Robert E. Lee, the noble icon of the Lost Cause. Each spring, KAs across the Southland celebrate the ultimate southern frat party, Old South, during which uniformed youths and hoop-skirted belles revel in the name of antebellum tradition and under the influence of Rebel Yell whiskey.

THE STARS AND BARS OF DIXIE

Playing tribute to the Old South also comes in more controversial forms, namely the song "Dixie" and the battle flag of the Confederacy, the Southern Cross. Seems somebody is always giving or getting a lot of flap about why so many folks down here still wave that flag and sing that tune after so many years.

Whether you look at them as the symbols of regional pride or as the up-to-no-good badges of twentieth-century Johnny Rebs, it's for sure these reminders of the Old South won't go away, away from Dixieland, any time soon. Seeing as they do belong to our heritage, you had better bone up on how they came to be a part of Southland culture.

"Dixie": The song that has been called "the doxology of the Southern religion of the lost cause," as well as "the best pep song ever written," actually was penned by a staunch Unionist, Daniel Decatur Emmett of Ohio, for a minstrel show in 1859. Soon "Dixie" was popular on both sides of the Mason–Dixon line, and it's even said that both presidents, Abe Lincoln and Jeff Davis, were partial to the lively tune which, to this day, never fails to cause a commotion when it's played.

Confederate flags: Above all, know that there's no such thing as a "rebel" flag or *the* Confederate flag. What you see in the Southland today (as commonly brandished by the if-your-heart-ain't-in-Dixie-get-your-ass-out set) is the Confederate battle flag, called the Southern Cross. One of *five* flags that Confederate States of America armies waved, it was never designated the official CSA flag. Although the Southern Cross might have been retired at Appomattox along with Lee's sword, it's still on active duty Down South.

CHAPTER THREE

Charm School, Southern Style

Why There's No Style Like Southern Style

No matter how brief your stay in Dixie, a basic proficiency in southern social customs will make your sojourn all the more delightful—and definitely more comprehensible. Spend more than a little time here, and you'll notice that the charming things we do in the spirit of Southernness have probably rubbed off on you. Stay a considerable duration, and you will realize that just when you thought you had the hang of our cultural conventions, Surprise! You find you still don't know grits from granola.

But don't lose heart. Everybody knows southern social nuance borders on the Byzantine. Just remember our rules of order from chapter 1, then proceed to today's lesson in Charm School, Southern Style. Sooner or later, your perseverance is bound to pay off.

DEPORTMENT DOWN SOUTH

Make no mistake about it: Manners matter in Dixie. You can be as poor as a church mouse or ugly as a mud fence, but don't ever be found empty-handed of good manners. They're the fixed price of admission into the fellowship of southern good folk.

Long before young Southerners can spell *black-eyed peas,* they're proficient at the rudiments of deportment, Southern Style. They know why they are, too, because:

1. The Bible says so (Don't forget the Golden Rule and setting a Christian example; this *is* the Bible Belt);
2. Good manners make life more pleasant for everybody;
3. Good manners are democratic ("Manners will get you where money won't");
4. Good manners are what make Southerners different (a euphemism for "better") from those who Aren't From Here, a distinction of which Southerners are *very* aware and *very* proud.

You simply can't take good manners too seriously Down South. While an occasional trifling with the law of southern manners can be tolerated (but not excused), those who blatantly defy it will soon find themselves about as warmly received as secular humanists or carpetbaggers. After all, we Southerners wrote the bible on good manners and believe in practicing what we preach.

■ **The Fundamentals of Good Manners**

Do you need to bring your manners up to snuff? These five fundamentals should set you in good stead. Just remember this first of all: Good manners are extended to everybody, regardless of whether you know them, on which side of town they live, or whether they tithe.

1. Be humble: Others first; yourself last. Self-denial and deference to others ("After you") are the cornerstone of good manners; acting selfish or uppity is not. This commandment is indisputably rooted in Bible Belt theology ("The first shall be last, and the last shall be first").

2. Be courteous: Remember the Golden Rule. Go out of your way to be helpful and kind to everyone you encounter ("Why, it wouldn't be no trouble a'tall to carry you on up to the Jitney Jungle, Miss Sally").

3. Behave yourself: Don't be uncouth, rude, brash, loud, coarse, or cause a commotion in public. Only trashy types and Yankees do such things . . . and obviously this is because they weren't raised to know better.

4. Be friendly: Put your friendliest foot forward, whether you've been properly introduced or don't know the person from a hole in the ground. Be sociable and neighborly, just like you learned in Sunday school ("Thou shalt love thy neighbor as thyself").

5. Be modest: Never be highfalutin'. Practice modesty in all situations. "Why, shucks, I guess I was in the right place at the right time" would work just fine upon learning that you had won the Pulitzer Prize. "Of course I won it, I deserved to" would absolutely categorize you as too big for your britches.

■ **Common Courtesies in Dixie**

Too much is never enough.

1. Say "please" without fail. Please, always say "Please" when you make a request, no matter how trivial or important.

2. Always ask, never tell. The only way to make a request is to ask for it; directives are much too surly. "Would you please carry me up the road a piece?" is correct. "Give me a ride to the market" is most assuredly not.

3. Say "Thank you" without fail. Upon being granted your request—be it a personal favor or impersonal transaction—always look the other party in the eye, give them a pleasing smile, and cheerily say, "Thank you." To show them you're really grateful, dress it up with "Thank you kindly," "Thanks a whole lot," "'Preciate it." If your request is denied, say, "Well, thank you anyway," using your best turn-the-other-cheek manner.

4. Say "ma'am" and "sir" without fail. If any adult your senior addresses you (or vice versa), automatically attach the appropriate title to your response ("Yes ma'am"; "I reckon so, sir"; "Pardon me, ma'am"). Neglecting this rule is apt to be interpreted as arrogance or insolence or just a plain bad upbringing.

5. Always refer to those of the female gender as ladies. The descriptive *woman* is usually reserved in Dixie for females of questionable respect. If you are a gentleman, then treat all ladies with the courtliness, deference, and respect you'd accord members of the royal family since, in the South, ladies occupy such status. This is an immutable rule of order in Dixie, no matter what may be happening elsewhere on this planet.

LADIES AND GENTLEMEN OF THE SOUTH

While good manners are the common denominator among southern good folk, some of our good folk represent the gold standard of social grace Down South: Southern Gentility. Part tradition, part Protestant ethic, part breeding, and a tad pretense (but can you blame us?), Southern Gentility is the ultimate state of social grace for a Southerner.

Membership in these august ranks of Southern Gentility earns you such designations as Southern Lady, Southern Gentleman, and Fine Young Lady/Man (the latter being generously applied to anyone not yet over the hill). It means you're a shining example of Southern Style, grace, charm, and propriety (no matter what or where the circumstances) and a living testament to the virtues of a respectable southern upbringing.

If you must ask, money has absolutely *nothing* to do with gentility. In fact, the reverse often applies. In a land where worldly possessions have frequently come and gone ("The Lord giveth and the Lord taketh away") over the last 130 years, Southern Gentility is defined by the ownership of the intangible. Money may buy privilege, but it won't get your big toe in the door when it comes to Southern Gentility.

Remember, "A good name is rather to be chosen than great riches." Amen.

■ Archetype of a Southern Lady

The Southern Lady is living proof of southern values and ideals. If you can't pass the following muster, you won't pass for a Southern Lady. The following attributes are standard equipment on the genuine article:

- Is a Southerner by birth who loves God, her family, and the Southland.
- Was brought up "right" (conservative, traditional, churchgoing) and raises her children the same way.
- College educated (state school; maybe private school if wealthy).
- Is a paragon of good taste, refinement, and prudence.
- Always looks presentable (wearing makeup, nice clothes, and simple jewelry)—even at home.
- Is gracious and accommodating; sugar-coats differences of opinion.
- Is adept at protecting the male ego; respects traditional sex roles.
- Is actively involved in volunteer work.

■ Archetype of a Southern Gentleman

Becoming a Southern Gentleman is the unwritten expectation, if not aspiration, for almost every son of the South. Joining the fellowship of this fraternal order of gentility is a long-

Charm School, Southern Style

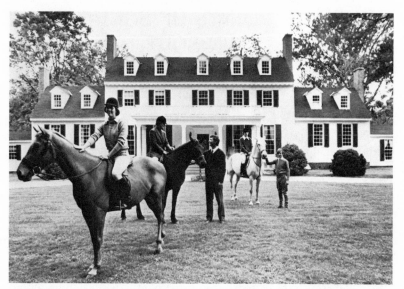

Riding at Sherwood Forest Plantation, Charles City, Virginia

standing rite of passage for a southern male, and few pass up the opportunity to belong. He:

- Is a Southerner by birth who loves God, his family, and the Southland.
- Was brought up "right" (conservative, traditional, churchgoing) and raises his children the same way.
- College educated.
- Is a paragon of good taste and manners.

- His word is his deed.
- Is gainfully employed in a respectable profession and lives a comfortable lifestyle.
- Takes a *very* traditional view of women's roles.
- Is a master at the social graces with women of all ages: courtesy, ceremony, flattery, wit.
- If imbibes, holds his liquor.
- Is a proficient outdoor sportsman (probably hunts or fishes often) and a team sports player or fan.

THE FINER POINTS OF SOCIAL SKILL DOWN SOUTH

Real ladies and gentlemen of the South observe hundreds of social dicta that far eclipse the please-and-thank-you variety. Mastering these finer points of distinction is all part of respecting your upbringing and the Southland.

■ No-No's for Ladies

A real southern lady knows better than to:

- Raise her voice or point her finger.
- Wear white shoes or carry a white purse before Easter Sunday or after Labor Day.
- Drink a gin and tonic if it's not warm weather.
- Shake hands when introduced in strictly social situations.
- Tell a betrothed lady "Congratulations" upon learning of her engagement. (Correct form is "best wishes"; after the ceremony, "congratulations" is proper.)
- Clean her plate when dining in public.

- Neglect her social correspondence, particularly thank-you notes for social niceties.
- Allow herself to be mentioned by the press on occasions other than birth, debut, marriage, and death.

■ Must-Do's for Gentlemen

Chivalry may not be well appreciated outside the South today, but you can be sure that around home territory a true gentleman will so honor a lady:

- Hold the door open for all members of the fairer sex, regardless of their social station.
- Stand when a lady enters or leaves the room.
- Walk on the streetside of a sidewalk when accompanying a lady.
- Order for the both of them when at a restaurant (excluding business meals).
- Always call his mother "Mama" or "Mutha"—never by her first name, no matter what his age.

THE SOUTHERN BELLE: MULTIPLE PERSONALITY

What image could be more ubiquitous to the Southland than that of a fetching Southern Belle? Why, her very silhouette—not to mention her reputation—is universally legend. She's the Diana of southern mythology, the Nefertiti of the Mississippi, the crown princess of Dixie. She's flirtatious, coy, and impossible to cipher. Her admirers are legion.

Despite her visible and lofty position, the modern Southern Belle defies definition. Such is the consequence of being a cultural icon: as her popularity grew, so did the interpretations of belledom. Nowdays there are multiple takes on the part of a Southern Belle although, mind you, each will insist hers is the only *authentic* version.

Herewith, the most prevalent:

■ The Blue-Blood Belle

A wealthy old-liner from a Deep South dynasty. Her numbers are especially concentrated around the Mississippi Delta region, where cotton aristocracy still presides. She's comely, quite the partier, and given to impetuous capers. She's educated and sophisticated, yet a threat to go barefoot. She revels in her privileged position and wears her identity like a crown. To her, being a blue-blood belle is like belonging to the world's most exclusive sorority.

■ The Heritage Belle

She's historian, scholar, and curator of the southern legacy. She keeps the flame of Southernness alive, not with burning crosses but candlelight open houses. She knows that ours is a remarkable past, and nothing short of the second coming of Christ will interfere with her efforts to preserve it for future generations.

■ The Beauty Belle

Pulchritude on parade. A lass with a southern accent who's made her good looks her life's calling. Loves to make a big impression; usually easy to do with all that makeup and big hair and a body dressed to kill. Exceptional candidates win beauty pageants, all the way to Miss America. Age knows no boundaries, for in her mind, a beauty belle never loses her allure—even when she's lost her youth.

■ The Tourism Belle

Commercially sanctioned version of the legend, these belles are strictly for show. Photogenic young ladies in hoop skirts are put on display in Old South settings. A necessary accessory for any halfway realistic antebellum depiction, these belles enchant tourists and help line the coffers of preservation. It's considered a position of honor to wear these hoops, and you'll find many a Beauty Belle aiding the cause.

■ The Hollywood Belle

Endless scenes of flouncing pantaloons and fits of petulance have reduced this belle to a simpering parody of her antebellum ancestors. She's the invention of Tinseltown and the epitome of cliché—flirtatious, flighty, spoiled—and today she's still standard fare when scripts call for a southern female.

PRETTY WOMEN IN DIXIE

True or false? "Southern women are just better looking."

Well, of course it's true. Ask anybody. Ask us: we've seen those contestants from the North and Midwest in the Miss America pageant, and we're not surprised in the least when they don't win.

Truth is, we just grow 'em prettier down here. What else would explain the fact that we *do* have a stupendous track record at big-time beauty pageants (and that we have scads of our own for all ages)? That per capita sales of makeup are higher in the South than anywhere else in the U.S.? That every southern girl aspires to be a cheerleader or majorette? That charm schools never fell out of favor with us? That some diehard college sororities still maintain standards for hair and makeup?

Face it: life Down South is one continuous beauty pageant. Ladies are expected to always look as pretty and fresh as a flower, no matter what the circumstances, which they do with confidence, skill, and a professional's vengeance. Pity the gal who's spied having a bad hair day. It would have been better for her not to leave the house, because she *will* be talked about—and she *will* be mortified. Believe it when you hear the story of the lady who dashed from her burning house with only her mascara and curling iron to her name, or the one about the lady who went to her grave without hubby ever seeing her *sans* makeup.

Such behavior is not viewed by us as unnecessary sacrifice or cultural poppycock. It's done in the line of duty. Because Southerners are special, you know. God ordained it. Which is why our women are just better looking—and it would certainly be a sin not to make the most of what God so generously gave our fairer sex.

A GOOD LOOK AT GOOD OLD BOYS

Some legends of the Southland actually do exist, none probably better known than the Good Old Boy. Yes, there are lots and lots of them Down South, *thriving.*

There are many dimensions to this business of the Good Old Boy. This is because almost all southern males have a touch of Good Old Boy in their blood, the only real difference being how much. Better get yourself acquainted with him now.

■ Basic Good Old Boy

The original, authentic model. Garden-variety, middle-class Southerner and contented to be one. A country boy at heart, if not in residence. Hard-working, good-hearted, very traditional. Loves to hunt and/or fish. Likes country music and hymn singing. Genuine and unpretentious, but dumb as a fox. *Universally regarded in Dixie as the living embodiment of basic southern values and ideals.*

■ Quasi-Good Old Boy

Usually found in southern cities. Adept at assuming the good-hearted-country-boy demeanor of the genuine article on occasion, but wouldn't be caught dead doing it for a living. Uses persona to demonstrate southern origins and allegiance. Wearing it is *de rigueur* for all-male outings (hunting, fishing, sports events, or drinking), when southern accents get so thick you could cut them with a knife.

■ Good Old Boys' Club/ Good Old Boyism

Down-South equivalent of all-male power brokering. Networking with a southern accent and without women, blacks, or anyone else who fails to meet their qualifications (male, white, and southern). This club has been operative as long as the Southland. Members only.

SOUTHERN STYLE #3: THE GOOD OLD BOY
It's deer-hunting season in Dixie.

Fluorescent orange safety vest.
In vest pockets: compass, Winchester
00 buckshot shotgun shells, TRE-BARK
face mask.

Sears flannel shirt.

In back of Bronco: flashlight, Tinks #69
doe in rut urine, rope, toilet tissue, Sweatt
Rifleman tree stand, Igloo cooler (contains
Coca-Cola, maybe a few brews for
celebrating, sandwiches, and candy bars),
water cooler, L. L. Bean down sleeping bag,
.243 ammunition using 90-grain Speer
handloads, Bushnell binoculars.

Insulated underwear.

12-gauge Remington pump shotgun (243
custom-built rifle on gun rack in truck).

Duckback TRE-BARK™ coveralls,
matching gloves and Buck hunting knife in
pockets.

Browning insulated waterproof boots
(eight-inch height).

A FEW WORDS ABOUT ECCENTRICITY IN DIXIE

Somewhere along the line, Southerners became associated with a decided predilection for eccentric behavior. To hear some folks Not From Here tell it, lapses in lucidity are conventional in Dixie, an unfortunate consequence of all that heat and humidity or generations of in-breeding. And it doesn't help matters, either, that an inordinate amount of southern literature and drama seems to contain at least one unforgettably eccentric character.

Well, it does so happen that some Southerners are more disposed than others to indulge their idiosyncrasies—even to the point of slightly bending the rules of social convention. But we will deny till we're blue in the face that there are more eccentrics per capita in Dixie than anywhere else on God's green earth.

The real difference lies in our attitude toward the subject. For most Southerners, an encounter with eccentric behavior is surely nothing to throw up your skirt and scream about. If otherwise refined individuals cross the outer reaches of conformity on occasion, so what? What's a little harmless eccentricity among family or friends?

For some Southerners, having an eccentric in the family can even carry a sort of reverse social cachet. After all, there *is* something downright fascinating about having a second cousin, twice-removed, who is given to spiritedly conducting the congregation in its hymn singing from his pew on the fourth row or an elderly aunt who has eleven cats with the same name.

Just because we have a healthy appreciation for our eccentrics in the Southland, however, does not mean that showstopping displays of eccentricity are to be found everywhere you turn in Dixie. To the contrary, most Southlanders don't qualify as eccentrics, and such behavior is definitely excluded from our approved codes of southern deportment. But since most of us know an eccentric who otherwise is a well-mannered, well-meaning Southerner, we're inclined to leave that little wrinkle in the social fabric unpressed.

CHOOSING OUR WORDS DOWN SOUTH

There's a lot to be said for the oral tradition of the Southland. And being a loquacious folk, we stand at the ready to oblige it anytime, anywhere.

Having a way with words is a treasured tradition Down South. Lending flair to routine goings-on and adding emphasis to serious subjects, it makes everything in between a sight more entertaining.

Our way with words is the difference between fair-to-middling and mighty fine, between plain Jane and plumb larraping. It accounts for why phrases like "I haven't seen you in a coon's age!" and "Don't that just get your gumption?" are as plentiful Down South as fleas on a dog's back. It's the reason we speak with a drawl that's as sweet as honey and as slow as molasses. It's why our politicians, preachers, and storytellers can captivate an audience faster than greased lightning.

Folks Not From Here usually don't know that our manner of speaking is a clear echo of Old World English, with figures of speech from Scotland, Ireland, Africa, and the West Indies folded into southern history. But it doesn't take them long to learn that speech is the spice of life in Dixie. No wonder those who taste our linguistic concoctions can't resist adding them to their diet. Sample for yourself the following how-to for putting our words in your mouth.

THE DIXIE DRAWL

The best way to acquire a southern accent is to hear one—over and over, from genuine southern natives—and to practice it, over and over. Before you start, though, keep in mind that there is no such thing as *the* southern accent. There are all sorts of variations to our celebrated drawl, such as the redneck twang, the Junior League lockjaw, and Lord knows how many regional renderings. All of them are bona fide sounds of the South.

You can, however, get your mouth off and running in our general direction if you keep a few points in mind.

■ **Speak musically**

When it comes to speech, every Southerner is a born musician. Let your voice rise up and down the musical scale as you talk and include both upward and downward inflections during the last word of your sentence.

■ **Don't rush**

What's your hurry? Let each syllable roll around in your mouth. Prolong the pleasure of monosyllabic words by stretching them out and adding inflections, as in transforming *Hi!* to *Hi-i-i-i!* and *down* to *dow-un-n-n.*

■ **Flatten out and distend your vowels**

Pay special attention to your *i*'s, *o*'s and *u*'s. For example, pronounce the *o* in *roll* the way you would in *ouch.*

■ **Avoid precisely enunciating all syllables in a word**

Just let the sounds ease out of your mouth; don't make work of it, for goodness' sake. When you can contract two syllables without a second thought as in revising *considerable* to *considerble*, then you've got it.

■ **Slur or drop an occasional ending consonant**

This is admirably exemplified by dropping the *g* from *ing* endings ("endins") and the *d* from *and* ("an").

■ **Pause thoughtfully between phrases**

Imagine you've liberally sprinkled commas and dashes throughout your sentences, as in "Well . . ." (long pause) "that situation . . ." (pause) "got me a little . . ." (pause) "flusterated."

DIXIE DICTION

Nobody can top a Southerner in turning a phrase. No other culture employs more figures of speech and inventive descriptives than we do in Dixie. Most are homegrown, and all will do to ride the river with. Why just communicate when you can expressivate Southern Style?

■ **Southern Lexicon**

Words no Southerner can do without:

Abide: tolerate, as in "I can't abide that place."

Act up: misbehave, as in "Her boys sure do like to act up."

Antsy: nervous, fidgety.

Biggety: conceited, full of oneself.

Bodacious: term of expansive approval or appreciation, as in "That's just plumb bodacious of you!"

Chew the fat: discuss, talk at length.

Conniption: fit of anger.

Druthers: preference, as in "If I had my druthers, I'd stay put."

Feisty: spirited, spunky.

Fetching: attractive, sexy.

Fired up: excited, motivated, as in "The Crimson Tide is all fired up to win!"

Fixing to: about to initiate action, as in "I'm fixing to go over to his house."

Gallivant: cavort, strut.

Give out: tire out.

Gumption: resolve, fortitude, as in "I don't know if she's got the gumption to do it."

Het up: mad, angry.

Hog wild: over-enthusiastic, out of control.

Larraping: delicious, tasty.

Mosey: amble about in no particular hurry, as in "I guess I'll mosey on home now."

No count: worthless.

Own up: confess.

Peart: perky, full of vim and vigor.

Piddling: insignificant thing or activity, as in "He's just piddling around in the yard."

Play pretties: trinkets.

Plumb: downright, absolutely, as in "Mama's plumb tuckered out."

Pooch: stomach bulge, as in "Jimmy's got himself a pooch from all that Dixie beer."

Puny: sickly, under the weather.

Put out with: aggravated, vexed.

Put up: set aside, prepare in advance, can or freeze.

Rambunctious: boisterous, disorderly.

Recollect: recall, as in "I recollect when your grandmama used to put up tomatoes like there was no tomorrow."

Riled up: angry.

Rot gut: strong, harsh liquor.

Ruckus: commotion, fight.

Sashay: strut, prance.

Scrounge: make something from nothing, scrape together, as in "I'll see if I can scrounge up some supper."

Shuck: take off.

Shucks: exclamatory term of regret, softcore cuss word.

Smidgin: a little bit.

Splavocate: blow up, explode, as in "I thought he was going to splavocate when she told him she wanted a divorce."

Stand-offish: haughty.

Stove up: bedridden, too ill to work.

Sweet talk: convince someone through flattery.

Swig: a gulp of drink, as in "Give me a swig of your Co-Cola."

Tacky: in bad taste, tawdry.

Tote: carry.

Traipse: trudge around, wander, as in "Odell had me traipsing all over town looking for that rocking chair."

Tuckered out: tired, exhausted.

Tump over: knock over, fall over.

■ Lessons in Locution

Or how to get your point across, Southern Style.

As naked as a jaybird.
As crazy as a bedbug.
As dead as a doornail.
As mean as a snake.
As thin as a rail.
As ugly as homemade sin.
As sharp as a tack.
As smart as a whip.
As blind as a bat.
As right as rain.
As crazy as a loon.
As ugly as a mud fence.
As mad as a hornet.
As wet as a drowned rat.
As limp as a dishrag.

As dry as a bone.
So ugly a train would jump the tracks.
Looks like something the cat drug in (bedraggled).
All bent out of shape; fit to be tied (angry, frustrated).
Like a chicken with its head cut off; all in a flap (agitated to the point of distraction).
Like a bat out of hell (in a hellfire hurry).
Get up a head of steam (work up momentum).
As rough as a cob (uncouth, roughneck).
As high as a cat's back (expensive).
As tight as a tick (miserly).
As scarce as hen's teeth.
Got a lot of gall (bold, presumptuous).
Fix his clock (retaliate).
My hind foot; in a pig's eye (I emphatically object).
In a coon's age; in a month of Sundays (a long time).
Down in the mouth (sad, despondent).
Like a duck on a June bug (without hesitation).
Stuck between a rock and a hard place (in a no-win situation).
Called on the carpet; taken to task (reprimanded).
He'd do to ride the river with (is reliable, trustworthy).
All by my lonesome.
Done done (finished).

THE USE OF *UP* IN SOUTHLAND SPEECH

That Southerners use the word *y'all* as if there was no tomorrow is not a revelation to most people. But you might be surprised to learn that we're partial to attaching the word *up* to our figures of speech. If you're around a Southerner, you'll hear what we mean in no time at all, since we like to tack the word onto the end of all sorts of verbs.

Sure, it's superfluous and has nothing to do with direction, but we just happen to like the lift it adds to our speech. Listen up to what we mean: "I'm going to fix us up some supper." "He needs someone to carry him up to the schoolhouse." "Those flowers sure did brighten up my day." "Get on up here, boy, before I break off your leg and beat you over the head with it." "Call up the office and tell them I'm running slow."

To speak Southern Style authentically, you'll need to spice up your speech with an occasional *up*. It's a subtle, but genuine, way to bring your speech up to par in Dixie.

TO TURN A PHRASE AND TELL A TALE IN DIXIE

Whether on podium, pulpit, printed page, stump, or street corner, Southerners are masters of rhetoric. Our gift for gab, spoken or written, is one of our most treasured resources. Few other places on earth can claim such a magnificent and respected legacy. Allow us to elaborate.

■ **Southern Literature**

Southern writers know no equal in their prowess with the narrative style. Classic examples abound in the works of William Faulkner, Eudora Welty, Flannery O'Connor, Thomas Wolfe, Truman Capote, Carson McCullers, and Taylor Caldwell, whose fiction is still compellingly potent:*

> Maycomb was an old town, but it was a tired old town when I first knew it. In rainy weather the streets turned to red slop; grass grew on the sidewalks, the courthouse

You'll find more literary muscle-flexing in chapter 4's "Voices of the Southern Experience."

sagged in the square. Somehow, it was hotter then: a black dog suffered on a summer's day; bony mules hitched to Hoover carts flicked flies in the sweltering shade of the live oaks on the square. Men's stiff collars wilted by nine in the morning. Ladies bathed before noon, after their three o'clock naps, and by nightfall were like soft teacakes with frostings of sweat and sweet talcum.

—Harper Lee,
To Kill a Mockingbird

■ Storytelling

Spinning yarns and swapping tall tales is anything but child's play in our neck of the woods. The more imaginative, convoluted, and longer-winded the better, and a sure hand on the humor doesn't hurt, either. Budding tellers practice on their relatives from an early age, then hone their craft over the fence post or a cup of coffee. The most talented can be found at regular gatherings in most southern locales and convening at open competitions. (The famed National Storytelling Festival in Jonesborough, Tennessee, is a three-day marathon of jawing.) May the best big mouth win.

■ Religion

The Bible Belt was stretched across the Southland with the impassioned exhortations of fundamentalist preachers. The civil rights movement was cradled in black southern churches, whose ministers inspired the making of history. The oral tradition is so embedded in the southern psyche that even the staidest of religious denominations are flavored with linguistic morsels during the delivery of the sermon. In many fundamentalist churches (particularly rural ones), rhetorical form is as important as content. To folks of these persuasions, dramatic oratory is regularly dished up in generous helpings.

■ Politics

Anyone who's ever attended a session of a southern state legislature, or even a hearing in town hall, knows that a podium affects a Southerner like waving a red flag does a bull. Given our innate tendency to loquacity and our belief that eloquence is a God-given gift, you can imagine how we relish a captive audience.

■ Prattle

Our proclivity to prattle at will is sometimes derided by critics as "garrulity," "stream of consciousness garble," or, at worst, "diarrhea of the mouth." This is hardly a kind thing to say about one of our favorite forms of self-expression. Agreed, prattle is by nature verbose and its content frequently inconsequential. But it *is* extraordinarily useful to its many practitioners. Not only is prattle a pleasant pastime and cheap entertainment, it's a reliable way to get things off our chests and to keep our jaws limber. Not bad, considering the price of admission.

WHAT'S IN A NAME DOWN SOUTH

Just as we Southerners are known for our gracious manners and distinctive style of speech, we're no less known for our singular names. Mind you, not all Southerners possess a classically Southern-style name, but you can be darn sure that somebody in their family does. And likely as not, at least one of them lives in a town with a name that indisputably belongs in the Southland.

Names are one more way we pledge allegiance to the South. They're as much a deep-down part of Dixie as kudzu, grits, and possums—and equally as unique.

■ **Names to Go By**

Double First Names: Always a popular option for either sex, both the first name (usually two syllables) and middle name (usually one syllable) are used in combination: Billy Wayne, David Earl, Tommy Lee, Jimmy Bob, Clara Jean, Edna Rae, Sadie Ruth, Pamela Georgeann, Nettie Mae, and Mary Margaret.

A and E Names: An amazing number of southern names end with a long *a* or *e* sound. Since Southerners have a penchant for ending their sentences with a lilt, this phenomenon is understandable. Examples: Maudie, Odessa, Loretta, Sadie, Lela, Hattie, Petie, Grady, Jonita, Alma, Leola, Jessie, Lanny, Willie, Callie, Ruby, Ida, Cassie, and, of course, Melanie and Ashley.

Bible Names: A standard source for southern names and a favorite of our older generations: Beulah, Esther, Joanna, Mark, Ruth, Obed, John, Joshua, Seth, James, Mary, Martha, Rachel, Andrew, and Caleb.

Multi-generational Names: Southern women make the same statement as men do with *Junior* and *III* after their names, only with a more down-home approach. The grandmother adds *Big* to her name (as in Big Mary Elizabeth), the mother goes by the given name (Mary Elizabeth), and the granddaughter gets *Little* in front of her name (yep, as in Little Mary Elizabeth).

Initials: Southern males, particularly those who share at least one name in common with their daddies, often elect to be known by the initials of their first two names, as in J. B., R. A., or K. T.

Surnames As First Names: A popular choice for old-line southern families. Parents bequeath their little ones with family surnames for first names, a socially approved way to brag on the family tree. Examples: Mackey, Sage, Lee, Avery, Ashley, Pinckney, Candler, Stuart, Winn, Dale, Blakely, Lane, and Bolling.

Classic Down-South Names: For some fitting examples of Southern Style at work, consider these classics: Myrtice, Lavinia, Ernest, Crystal, Luther, Shirlene, Eunice, Lester,

Jonita, Everette, Buck, Lula, Loretha, Etta Faye, Bernice, Buddy, and Bubba (the last two, our famous corruptions of the word *brother*).

Terms of Endearment: Sugar puddin', precious lamb, darlin', cuteness, honey child, sweetness, and sweet thing.

■ Name That Town

Clearly our southern ancestors had a fair share of whimsy when they named our towns; there are more memorable place names across Dixie than Quaker has oats. Some of the best examples of their handiwork, below, should give you more than an eyeful of evidence.

What You See Is What You Get: Muscadine, Petal, Leaf, Grapevine, Tomato, Dewy Rose, Pine Log, Burnt Corn, Pearl, Duck Hill, Turtletown, Hill, Locust Grove, Doe Hill, Bat Cave, Burnt Corn, Turkey Creek, Birdsnest, Flat Rock, Cut Off, Big Flat, Oil Trough, Talking Rock, Six Mile, Ten Mile, Hard Cash, Hot Coffee, Midnight, Piney Woods, Ozone, Smut Eye, and Slapout.

Biblical and Inspirational Names: Shiloh, Goshen, Antioch, Corinth, Uriah, Joppa, Beulah, Mordecai, Berea, Friendship, Benevolence, Reliance, Faith, Grace, Excel, Learned, Fair Play, Harmony, Success, and Prosperity.

Just Plain Strange Names: Eclectic, Normal, Enigma, Nuttsville, Chance, Ball Ground, Hytop, Experiment, Ty Ty, Pooler, Iuka, Kokomo, Lux, Nitta Yuma, Whynot, Soso, Many, Iota, Eastabuchie, Davy Crockett, Ivanhoe, Hortense, Old Joe, Apex, Climax, Hustle, Ether, Husk, Stem, Shongaloo, Jigger, Mayo, Peedee, Finger, Bland, Gore, Nail, Trussville, Extension, Dry Prong, Smackover, and Frankewing.

CHAPTER FOUR

Made in Dixie

A Slew of the Southland's Outstanding Claims to Fame

There's a whole slew of things, places, and faces that we make a proud claim to in the Southland (plus a few we make do with). Not only are they the sights and sounds of life, Southern Style, we're happy to note that they're often a slice of life, American style—probably more often than you ever imagined.

To see for yourself what this bragging is all about, keep on reading. We predict you'll be mightily impressed once you see for yourself what it means to be made in Dixie. So welcome to our southern world as God made it and we've arranged it.

Graceland, home of Elvis Presley

THE GOD-GIVEN AND THE GOD-FORSAKEN

■ God-Given

Magnolias: The quintessence of the Old South, *Magnolia grandiflora* is a native Southerner. Each summer, when the large, milky white blossoms of this broadleaf evergreen unfold and fill the air with their sweet fragrance, folks all over Dixie lapse into momentary states of euphoria, nostalgia, and blissful content.

Dogwoods: A blooming dogwood is a Southerner's assurance that spring has indeed arrived. For some southern cities (most notably, Knoxville, Atlanta, and Birmingham), the rites of spring focus upon a Dogwood Festival, celebrated amidst a fairyland profusion of white and pink dogwoods. Dogwoods have assumed a place in Bible Belt lore, too; their four-petal blossoms are viewed as a timely symbol of Jesus' crucifixion.

Azaleas: Phooey on those scrawny bushes outside the Southland that masquerade as azaleas. You have to come to the Southland to see how God intended azaleas to look, and there's no better location than the acidic soil of the South's coastal plains. In cities like Mobile, Alabama, or Wilmington, North Carolina, azalea mania takes over each spring as massive banks of pink and fuchsia flowers transform the landscapes. In Mobile, a pink stripe is even painted on a thirty-seven-mile route of streets with the showiest arrays.

Spanish Moss: Sightings of Spanish moss, those gray, tufted strands that languidly hang from trees in warmer southern climes, tend to have the same effect on Southerners as magnolia blooms. Spanish moss compels you to cease all activity in favor of a nap under its host tree and to thank the good Lord you're a Southerner. Even its name is mysteriously romantic; so who cares that Spanish moss is not a moss at all, but a member of the pineapple family?

Kentucky Bluegrass: The mere mention of those two words gets plenty of Southerners plumb excited. Kentucky Bluegrass bespeaks an idyllic region and lifestyle, of southern gentry and gentility. The Bluegrass means rolling, grassy hills tinted a bluish hue in springtime, white-fenced pastures, the thrill of horse breeding and racing at its finest, and the pride of these Southerners who call it home.

Pecans: The nutmeat of the *Carya olivaeformis* tree, native to the Southland, is a favorite treat of folks everywhere. What would life be without pralines, pecan pie, and fruitcakes, to name but a few of the delights it's inspired? Hopefully, you're lucky enough to have a pecan tree in your yard or know someone who does. If you're out of luck, then run over to the closest co-op or farmers' market in the fall or place your mail order with pecan growers in the Deep South (see chapter 6).

Kudzu gone hog wild

Tobacco: The New World explorers weren't long in discovering the pleasurable properties of this southern nightshade plant. Since then, consuming tobacco has been a popular vice the world over. Some forms are largely consumed in Dixie; many a southern granny and grandpappy have been fond of a pinch of snuff ("to clear the mind"), while a plug of chewing tobacco is a close friend to many a good old boy. The first southern aristocracy was born from the profits of growing tobacco, and it's an enterprise in which the Southland still leads the pack worldwide (so to speak).

Cotton: Even though cotton isn't native to the Southland and we no longer lead the nation in its cultivation, at one time cotton was king in Dixie and altered the course of our history. The South's long growing season, the invention of the cotton gin (by a Yankee in Georgia), and worldwide demand for cotton textiles put the South on the map as a nineteenth-century exporter and poured millions of dollars into the plantation economy (at the height of the antebellum period, more than half of the nation's millionaires were cotton-rich Southerners). However, the wealth was controlled by relatively few and at the cost of freedom for many. King Cotton was reined in by the War, later again by the Great Depression and the boll weevil. Unless you're traversing the Mississippi Delta, don't count on seeing endless cotton fields in Dixie these days, even though acreage doubled between 1989 and 1991. Maybe you should look for soybeans instead.

■ God-Forsaken

Kudzu: Kudzu is an everpresent reminder to Southerners that some-

---

Dixie Vermin

Chiggers (Redbugs) • *Gnats*
Yellow Flies • *Mosquitoes* • *Fire Ants*
Roaches (Palmetto Bugs) • *Ticks*

---

times even we can have too much of a good thing. About fifty years ago, the oriental weed kudzu was hailed as the panacea for widespread soil erosion in Dixie. The erosion was checked, but the kudzu spread like wildfire over hill and dale and anything else in its path. The result is now a common sight in the Southland: ghostly topiary gardens of kudzu, where the vines have blanketed hillsides and enveloped structures. With a growth rate of up to sixty feet a season, you'd be wise not to stand still too long if you're close to kudzu.

Fire Ants: Since its stowaway arrival on a Mobile-bound freighter in 1918, this aggressive pest has steadily infested southern lands. Most Southerners have learned the hard way that disturbing the fire ants' formidable mounds will provoke the wrathful stings of several members of their 150,000-strong colonies. With so many of the tenacious little buggers now settled across the Southland, the fire ant is forever a resident of Dixie. Watch your step.

Roaches: It's our warm and humid climate that enables cockroaches to grow large (up to two inches) and in great abundance in Dixie. Sometimes delicately called "palmetto bugs" by Southerners, roaches invariably are residents of even the most well-kept southern households. Predictably, they make their appearances at socially inopportune times; but nothing short of torching a house will deter them (you can *forget* total extermination). House guests who spot a venturesome cockroach in a Dixie household are advised to grin and ignore the matter.

Climate: Sometimes the summer heat and humidity in Dixie become a sight uncomfortable, even for us Southerners. It gets pretty hot (expect afternoon highs to reach at least 90°) and mighty humid (coastal cities average over 80 percent humidity in the early mornings) during that long summer stretch. Since we prefer bare feet to cold any day of the week, we've learned to manage just fine. Besides, we reap our rewards with a very long crop-growing season, and when winter finally does arrive, we can rest assured it won't wear out its welcome.

DIVINELY INSPIRED LEGENDS

■ Gone With the Wind

It took Atlanta newspaper reporter Peggy Mitchell nearly ten years to complete her epic tale of the fall of the Old South and its painful rejuvenation. Were it not for the urging of her associates, a visiting New York book publisher in search of the Great Southern Novel would never have learned of her manuscript. The rest is history—of the grandest kind.

Six months after its June 30, 1936, publication, an astounding million copies of *Gone With the Wind* had been sold, despite its then unheard of price of three dollars (many folks pooled their change to afford a pass-around copy of the novel). By May of the following year, Margaret Mitchell had been awarded the Pulitzer Prize for her 1,037-page masterpiece and Hollywood was well on its way to creating the motion picture version. The world's perception of the Southland had become forever intertwined with the best-selling American novel of its time.

Vivian Leigh as Scarlett O'Hara

SOUTHLAND LOWDOWN ON
GONE WITH THE WIND

Not only is *Gone With the Wind* one of the best sellers of all time, many of its admirers believe it's also one of the most misunderstood. Commonly thought to be a dramatic eulogy for the antebellum South, it *did* indeed look back. But Margaret Mitchell's *Gone With the Wind* was more a command to look forward to a New South, with a new culture and new traditions.

Her message was personified in the quandary of Scarlett O'Hara who, like many Southerners, was torn between her ties to the Old South (symbolized by Tara and Ashley Wilkes) and her will to move onward and upward. Scarlett O'Hara did manage to overcome her circumstances, but she had to cast aside the old ways to do it and she paid a price to do so.

Through *Gone With the Wind*, Peggy Mitchell advised the twentieth-century Southland to do the same, but she didn't win many converts. It was a distant notion for most of the book's far-flung audience, and needless to say, the Old Guard was less than enthusiastic about taking her advice (and from one of its own, no less).

■ Coca-Cola

No product is more widely sold or recognized in the entire world than Coca-Cola, whose origin lies in the heart of the New South. About two billion ounces of the beverage are consumed daily in more than 135 countries; its parent company spends more than $150 million annually to advertise Coca-Cola and its sister beverages. Originally concocted in 1886 by Atlanta pharmacist John Pemberton (in a kettle in his back yard) for sale at soda fountains, the Coca-Cola business was bought out five years later by another pharmacist and entrepre-

neur, Asa Candler, for a total investment of $2,300. Mr. Candler knew what to do with a good thing when he saw it. By 1919 his family was able to sell the business for $25 million.

Despite turn-of-the-century flap about the presence of cocaine in its formula (small traces were found until 1905), Coca-Cola has long been a symbol of the wholesome, all-American life. Bottling plants accompanied American troops (at General Dwight D. Eisenhower's request) during World War II to boost soldier morale. Coca-Cola's advertising has mirrored America's culture almost as long as it has been around. Behind the wholesome product, however, is a very sophisticated parent company and network of bottlers that takes an aggressive stance to defy competitors (especially archrival Pepsi-Cola) and imitators ("spies" from the company's Trade Research Department sample the product in all corners of the world to "protect its integrity" as the Real Thing).

Coca-Cola coupon, 1890s

WHEN COKE LOST ITS FIZZ

A few summers ago the Coca-Cola Company got tangled up in its own britches: It shelved master Formula 7X for a new one. New Coke had arrived; "Old" Coke was gone. Despite the big ballyhoo created for its advent, it was hardly an auspicious debut. In less than three months an outraged public and dismal sales of the New Coke had convinced company executives to revive the much-loved Coke of old. New Coke, a hopeful head-on competitor for the smoother tasting Pepsi, was quickly flanked by its predecessor, to the audible relief of Coke bottlers and consumers. A sacred slice of Americana had been returned, but only after its parent corporation had eaten a big serving of crow.

■ Grand Ole Opry

The Southland is the birthplace of country music, and without a doubt the Grand Ole Opry is country music's cradle and homestead. From its 1925 start as the "WSM Barn Dance" in Nashville, Tennessee, when eighty-year-old Uncle Jimmy Thompson played fiddle for an hour to his niece Eva's piano accompaniment, the Opry has been the world's longest-running live radio show. Performers like Roy Acuff, Minnie Pearl, Hank Williams, Patsy Cline, George Jones, Buck Owens, Dolly Parton, Tammy Wynette, Porter Wagoner, and Johnny Cash have entertained millions of loyal listeners each Saturday evening with the strains of country music and its musical cousins.

From 1943 to 1974, disciples of the Opry filled the hard wooden pews of Ryman Auditorium, a former gospel tabernacle; the Opry now convenes in the modern Grand Ole Opry House at Opryland USA's fancy complex, also home base for a 120-acre theme park, a hotel, and The Nashville Network's television facilities.

■ Bourbon Whiskey

Bourbon is the South's own firewater and has been for more than 350 years since early Virginia settlers brewed corn and maize to lift their homesick spirits. Three years before Kentucky was admitted to the Union in 1789, the Reverend Elijah Craig was distilling corn whiskey there; eighty years later, Tennessean Jack Daniel took the whole process one step further, with charcoal mellowing the amber

liquid to create Tennessee sour mash whiskey and allowing a somewhat smoother sip.

Whether you're high-class, good old folk, or white trash, if you're southern and you drink hard liquor, you love whiskey. Whiskey drinking is firmly fixed in southern culture. Some even liken bourbon, in its brashness and vigor, to the South itself. We won't disagree.

■ Mint Juleps

Is there a libation more southern than the genteel mint julep? No, least not one that isn't drunk straight from the bottle. And isn't it true that all we do Down South is sit on the veranda and sip our mint juleps? No, but it is true that you can buy them at the mint julep concession when you attend the Kentucky Derby. As for concocting them at home, recipes abound, all variations on a legendary theme. Should you not have one committed to memory, this recipe should put some genuine South in your mouth:

Original Kentucky Mint Julep Recipe

Put 12 sprigs fresh mint in bowl, cover with powdered sugar and just enough water to dissolve the sugar. Crush with wooden pestle. Place half the crushed mint and liquid in the bottom of a crackled glass tumbler or in sterling silver tankard. Fill glass half full of finely crushed ice. Add rest of crushed mint and fill remainder of glass with crushed ice. Pour in whiskey until glass is brimming. Place in ice box for at least an hour, preferably two or three hours, if you can wait that long. Decorate with sprigs of mint covered with powered sugar when ready to serve.

—reprinted with permission from *The Cooking Book,* The Junior League of Louisville

■ *Southern Living* **Magazine.**

Every coffee table worth its salt in Dixie carries an issue of *Southern Living* magazine, the monthly house, garden, and travel epistle "For people who love the South." *Southern Living* is an institution of high regional regard; it's Southern Gentility in print. Conservative, refined, traditional, and never controversial, it exudes faith and confidence in Southernness and serves as a guide to southern pursuits ("The Long and Short of Okra," "Riding in the Ozarks").

The magazine is such an unavowed success (now well over two million prosperous subscribers) that Time, Inc., purchased it and its sister publications (including *Progressive Farmer*) in 1985. The Yankee purchase prompted warnings of canceled subscriptions by a few worried Southerners, but fortunately this is one thing Northerners have had the good sense to leave be.

■ **Country Hams**

What the Virginia settlers learned from the Indians about dry-curing meat soon became one of the Southland's best-known gastronomic pleasures: country hams. By rubbing pork with salt and smoking it, the colonists began a savory, 350-year-old tradition that is admired and revered. Although some rural Southerners still cure their own hams (including "Today" show weatherman Willard Scott), most of the delicacies come from a handful of respected producers. Highest on the hog of branded hams are those from Smithfield, Virginia (law requires that they are produced within the city limits), where four makers supply these famous smoked hams with the long-cut shanks.

Some ham makers swear by the smoking process (especially in humid coastal locations), using hardwoods such as apple, oak, and hickory; but around the Appalachians they vow that's just a lot of hot air. In either case, there's no ham like a southern country ham, and no breakfast like a southern breakfast with country ham and biscuits.

■ **Tennessee Walking Horses**

The horse with the springy "rocking chair" canter is the pride and joy of Middle Tennessee. Bred for more than 100 years, the high-stepping, overstepping Tennessee Walking Horse once provided plantation owners with a fast and comfortable ride over long distances; today, forest rangers and the Canadian Mounted Police follow suit. Most of these agreeable, dignified pleasure horses are bred and trained around Shelbyville, Tennessee, home of the Tennessee Walking Horse National Celebration (late August) when more than 1,600 walkers perform. The International Grand Championship in nearby Murfreesboro (early August) kicks off the annual excitement for the distinguished Tennessee Walking Horse's devotees.

■ Tabasco Sauce

The little bottle and its fiery contents have been relished worldwide for more than 125 years. In befitting style, Tabasco Sauce has lived an exotic life, lending zest to meals during the excavation of the tomb of Tutankhamen and even on Skylab. The legend began on Avery Island in southern Louisiana when Edmund McIlhenny chopped a special variety of peppers, blended them with vinegar and salt, and then aged them in wooden barrels. From the first 350 bottles, Tabasco Sauce was a success; within three years, the family had opened an office in London to handle foreign demand for the condiment. To this day Tabasco Sauce remains a family proposition, and a distinguished one at that, as a branch of the McIlhenny family is descended from twelfth U.S. president Zachary Taylor.

■ Cabbage Patch Kids

Once upon a time there was a North Georgia good old boy named Xavier Roberts who stitched together some pudgy-faced, cuddly dollies. He called his friends the Little People and found adoptive homes for them. Very soon, children around the South were visiting Mr. Roberts's Babyland General Hospital in Cleveland, Georgia, to adopt their very own Little People.

Before long a big toy maker decided girls and boys all over the world should have Little People of their own. The doll-babies' names were changed to Cabbage Patch Kids, and the toy maker found happy homes for close to fifty million of them. Not only has this made lots of children very happy, it's made Mr. Roberts, the toy maker, and other folks very wealthy.

■ Moon Pie

If you're a Southerner you can't say *Moon Pie* without grinning. First of all, even the name is amusing (inspired by a salesman who declared the world needed a cookie that was marshmallow, drenched in chocolate, and "as big as the moon"). Second, the confection itself is a funny-looking, hamburger-shaped thing made of cake, sugar, and marshmallow goo and coated in chocolate. Then there's the Moon Pie's humble reputation to consider: together with an RC Cola, it was once the Down-South equivalent of a plowman's lunch.

Despite its less than glamorous image, the Moon Pie is such a part of the Dixie heritage that Southerners are as fond of them as Northerners are of bagels. They've even made their way into Mardi Gras tradition, when parading revelers toss armfuls of the sandwiches to eager crowds who happily holler, "Moon Pie! Moon Pie!"

DIVINELY INSPIRED TRADITIONS

■ Mardi Gras

America's own version of pre-Lenten carnival cuts loose for two weeks each year in two southern port cities, Mobile and New Orleans, culminating on Shrove (or "Fat") Tuesday (*mardi gras* in French). Schools and businesses close the last two days before Lent, when the final hours of misrule reach a frenzied climax of parades, balls, parties, and generally sanctioned misbehavior. Even the usually hard and fast codes of southern conduct are relaxed in the name of revelry, much of which occurs behind the anonymity of masks and costumes.

Residents of both cities regularly debate whose observance began first, but most will allow that the first Mardi Gras society was formed in Mobile in 1830 by a group of young and inebriated carousers who dubbed themselves "The Cowbellion de Rakin Society" in honor of their noisemakers (cowbells, rakes, hoes). In both cities citizens take full advantage of the event, toasting the joys of excess in anticipation of Lenten penance. If you've ever participated, you know for a fact that Mardi Gras is a two-week party with the intensity of Saint Patrick's Day and the Super Bowl combined.

At the heart of the Mardi Gras tradition are the socially elite mystic societies (the older, the greater their prestige), whose parades entertain thousands of revelers. Their courts—kings and queens, knights, ladies in waiting, and so forth, who are presented in regal coronations—represent the cities' oldest and most prominent families.

Mardi Gras mystiks on parade, Mobile, Alabama

79

MARDI GRAS LEXICON

Words every reveler should know.

Krewe/Crewe: Refers to a carnival organization (also called a mystic society) and its merry-making membership. The idea was inspired by a John Milton masque play and first used by New Orleans's Mystick Krewe of Comus in 1857.

Bal masque: Masquerade ball. Every bona fide mystic society has one. Only members have the privilege of wearing costumes and masks. Dress for guests (invitation only) is *de rigueur,* ball gowns for ladies, white tie and tails for men, without exception.

Tableau: A dramatic scene assembled for use at a Mardi Gras ball, coronation, or parade float. Tableaux usually reflect a given theme, such as "Land of Make Believe," which has been selected by its mystic society for a particular year.

Dasante: Dinner dance given in honor of Mardi Gras royalty. Imagine a seated wedding dinner *sans* bride and groom and with a king and queen and Mardi Gras theme instead. Need we say more?

Serpentine: Colorful fettucini-thin streamers of paper that come in rolls and are unfurled in great quantities at Mardi Gras parades and celebrations.

Doubloon: Coins that bear the insignia of a given mystic society and are tossed by their float-riding members to parade-goers.

Flambeaux: Kerosene-fueled torches that are carried by lackeys to light the routes of night parades (artificial lighting is considered bad form).

■ **The Masters**

The enduring legacy of southern gentleman and golf great Bobby Jones is the Masters Golf Tournament. Played each April at the Augusta (Georgia) National Golf Club, the Masters began as an invitation tournament for Mr. Jones and a few of his buddies and is the only pro golf tournament to be played annually in the same location. The Masters has always been peerless. But considering that Bobby Jones and cohort Clifford Roberts were experienced savants of Southern Style, it was inevitable that the Masters would become synonymous with golf's finest.

Its course design has become a world standard for both challenge and beauty, and the most respected names

Annual "run for the roses" at the Kentucky Derby

in golf and society constitute its membership (even former president Dwight Eisenhower had a cottage on the grounds). No sporting event is more genteel than the Masters, where gentlemanly protocol and southern hospitality have made all the difference for the game of golf.

■ **The Kentucky Derby**

The world again looks southward (this time in Louisville, Kentucky) on the first Saturday each May, when the prestigious Run for the Roses kicks off the Triple Crown of horse racing. Modeled after the Epson Derby in England, the venerable Kentucky Derby has run with a high profile since 1875, and you can bet your last wager that Kentuckians intend never to lose this distinction. To the horse-racing community, the one-and-one-half-mile race is the ultimate test of mettle for three-year-old colts. To the Bluegrass State, it's a claim to fame *par excellence.*

To racegoers, the Derby is the undisputed crown social event. If your bluegrass roots are also blue-blooded, you can watch the event from Millionaire's Row atop the clubhouse and rub elbows in high style. If your social standing doesn't qualify you for the boxes or grandstand, you can still attend the race, as long as you're willing to share the infield with more than 70,000 other Derbygoers and arrive for the 5:00 P.M. event nine or ten hours early.

DIVINELY INSPIRED LEGACIES

■ **Southern Legacy #1:
Music-making in Dixie**

When the good Lord measured out musical inspiration, he must have dropped the bucket on the Southland, because we've certainly grown a bumper crop of musical traditions in Dixie. Surely nowhere else on this earth can rightly claim to be the birthplace of so many kinds of music, especially with such widespread appeal. We Southerners are naturally pleased to own this distinction, and we gladly put our money where our mouths are.

The music made in Dixie is the music of Everyman, the kind you can clap your hands to, tap your feet to, sway to, and maybe shed a tear to. You don't have to get too gussied up to listen to it, and you don't have to put on cultured airs (save them for when the symphony is in town). You just have to listen and enjoy yourself, maybe even join right in.

We Southerners are definitely old hands at making music, and no wonder. Our musical heritage came along with our forebears to the Southland. With so many musically minded cultures settling across Dixie, it was inevitable that we'd have enough songs in our hearts to beat the band, as the following will attest:

Traditional Folk Music: The folk music of the Southland hails from our Scottish-Irish and English ancestors, who settled in the mountains of the upland South. There, folk music came to be truly a family affair. Stories were handed down in ballads like "Barbara Allen" and "Pretty Polly" to fiddle and dulcimer accompaniments, while good old fiddle tunes ("Sallie Gooden") enlivened the tradition. Today the heritage of folk music continues to be passed from one generation to the next. Its legacy rings loud and clear in another southern-grown musical style, country music.

Gospel music: No old-time religion camp meeting was complete without plenty of harmonizing hymn singing, taught by traveling evangelists and singing-school teachers. To this day, gospel songfests abound across Dixie. Praising the Lord, gospel style, ranges from the traditional (old-time four-part hymns, anthems, and ballads) to the enthusiastic (call-and-response shouting) to the bluesy (spirituals). With the musical ministrations of gospel luminaries like the Speer Family, Mahalia Jackson, the Bill Gaither Trio, and Andre Crouch, gospel music has developed a large and faithful following, both inside and outside the Southland.

Cajun: South Louisiana's Cajuns are known for their robust and expressive lifestyle, and that includes their music. A melting pot of French, Creole, Celtic, and Anglo-Saxon influences, Cajun music is usually played with an accordion ("squeeze box"), fiddle, and triangle. Sometimes you sing or whoop ("Aiyee!!"); Sometimes you don't. But in either case, you most certainly dance to Cajun music, usually with a waltz or a two-step ("special"), and you should always *laissez les bons temps rouler* ("let the good times roll").

Blues: The powerful, soulful blues form of music was born in the Mississippi Delta region, a legacy that evolved from plantation work calls and musical ballads. Southern blacks created and nurtured the blues, which recall the frustration and melancholy of life and love, past and present. It didn't take long for blues music to attract a die-hard audience, once the Father of the Blues, W. C. Handy, published such classics as "Memphis Blues" and blues singers like Ma Rainey and others were recorded. It's true that the growing blues culture picked up steam for a while in Chicago, but the best blues you'll ever hope to hear still comes from the Southland, most notably in Memphis and points southward on the Delta.

W. C. Handy statue in Memphis, Tennessee

Jazz: We wouldn't go so far as to claim that Dixie was the birthplace of jazz, since not even musicologists can precisely settle that trivia question. But we can rightly claim that jazz was pretty much made in Dixie, since the cradle of jazz was most certainly rocked in New Orleans and most of jazz's greatest names are Southerners. Surrounded by the varied musical cultures of the Crescent City—black work songs, spirituals, the music of France and Spain (both were former mother countries of New Orleans), blues, and ragtime—the jazz band assumed its sound and lineup (rhythm, brass, and reed instruments). Under the inspiration of jazz greats and Southerners all—King Oliver, "Jelly Roll" Morton, Louis Armstrong, Dizzy Gillespie, and Bessie Smith—it didn't take long for this musical form to gain international acclaim.

Country: Country music is the southern psyche in song, our own homegrown style of storytelling and music-making with the southern experience written all over it. Country music was truly made in Dixie, the offspring of such southern musical parentage as folk music, early blues, vaudeville, parlor songs, and old-time religion. Led by its founding family, Virginia's Carter Family ("Will the Circle Be Unbroken?"), and the "Father of Country Music," Mississippi's Jimmie Rodgers, country music struck a familiar chord to its Dixie listeners. Once most Southerners could afford a radio or a Victrola, country music hit its stride and, by the 1930s, country music had taken the Southland, the Midwest, and the West by storm. Since then its appeal has built steadily and shows no sign of letting up.

It's not surprising that more than 80 percent of all country-western radio stations are in the South and Southwest. Don't forget, darlin', those songs are *our* songs. You have to possess the Down-South heritage to fully appreciate songs like "If You Don't Quit Checkin' on Me (I'm Checkin' Out on You)" or "Stand on My Own Two Knees," and you have to understand the country boy lifestyle, even if you don't affiliate. In a land where the American Dream runs as thick as fleas on a dog's back, country music stardom is proof positive that a good old boy or gal can do swell. By gumption, just look at what Loretta Lynn (the coal miner's daughter), Tammy Wynette (hairdresser), or Merle Haggard (mechanic) did with their God-given talents and a heck of a lot of determination, thanks to country music.

Bluegrass: While today country music is pretty much an electrified, fancified version of its earlier forms, the old-time pickin' and fiddlin' music of hillbilly string bands has anything but faded away. It's been thriving as bluegrass music since the 1940s, when Kentucky mandolin player Bill Monroe, the "Father of Bluegrass Music," and Earl Scruggs, a North Carolina banjo picker, first put together the classic bluegrass sound: fiddle, rhythm guitar, bass, five-string banjo, and mandolin.

If you've not had the pleasure of hearing bluegrass music, just remember the theme to the television show "The Beverly Hillbillies," particularly the end, when nimble pickers Lester Flatt and Earl Scruggs really got wound up (that's called a breakdown). Then you'll know why folks refer to bluegrass as "country music in overdrive." Lively, infectious, and good, clean fun, bluegrass music is a favorite musical style in Dixie. Hear some for yourself at summertime bluegrass festivals all across the Southland (see chapter 9), and you'll be hooked.

Rock and Roll: The roots of rock and roll are firmly planted in Dixie, reaching deep down into our black culture's rhythm and blues music. Southerners like Fats Domino and Little Richard crossed the staunch color barriers with their gutsily controversial music and set the stage for rock and roll's official arrival in 1955, when Tupelo, Mississippi, truck driver Elvis Presley turned the music world on its ear with the national hit "Baby, Let's Play House." From that day forward, rock and roll was here to stay, a dynamic derivative of rhythm and blues, country, and gospel music, all mainstays of the southern musical repertoire. Modern music has not been the same since.

ELVIS: "THE KING OF ROCK AND ROLL"

His gyrating hips created such a scandal that he was shown only from the waist up on the "Ed Sullivan Show," and his lyrics were equally suggestive to an audience more accustomed to Doris Day and Eddie Fisher. Both only fanned the fires of adoration by his teenage fans. Almost single-handedly Elvis Presley put sex and spunk into mainstream radio and inspired musicians throughout America and Britain to do the same.

The King of Rock and Roll ruled the pop, country, and rhythm and blues airwaves in the mid-to-late fifties. Classic hits like "Hound Dog," "Heartbreak Hotel," and "Love Me Tender" sold more than one billion records in his lifetime. Not bad for a thin-eared Mississippi boy who was born and raised to do without.

As the well-known story goes, Elvis's musical kingdom shrank as the King turned to making broad appeal pop music and white-bread movies (some Elvis students blame this on his manager, Colonel Tom Parker). Despite a brief comeback ("In the Ghetto," "Suspicious Minds"), the King's domain was reduced to flashy Las Vegas-style shows across the heartland of America. The man who died in 1977 at age forty-two, apparently from complications caused by drug abuse, was but a bloated caricature of the young man who took the throne of musicdom.

FIVE OF THE BIGGEST-SELLING COUNTRY MUSIC SINGLES EVER

"Bouquet of Roses" (1948), by Eddy Arnold
"I'm Movin' On" (1950), by Hank Snow
"Sixteen Tons" (1955), by Tennessee Ernie Ford
"Crazy Arms" (1956), by Ray Price
"Stand by Your Man" (1968), by Tammy Wynette

Courtesy of the Country Music Foundation

GRACELAND: HOME SHRINE OF THE KING

As far as the pop culture of the Southland is concerned, Elvis is as good as canonized. Just pay a visit to the King's home, Graceland (in Memphis), along with more than half a million others who arrive each year, to see what we mean.

In a Hollywood version of the southern plantation house pilgrimage, you can join throngs of reverent, die-hard Elvis fans for a tour of the mansion (filled with such arcana as giant stained-glass peacocks and a nine-foot grand piano covered in twenty-four-karat gold) and view his grave ("He was a precious gift from God") in the Meditation Garden. Be sure to take lots of Kleenex. Graceland is for grieving the loss of the King, and there's a lot of weeping and wailing and gnashing of teeth going on by despondent fans. End your mournful moments in the shops across the street from Graceland, where you can soothe your aching heart with Elvis memorabilia (don't forget the Love Me Tender hair conditioner).

If you're a true fan of the King's, you've probably already been to Graceland. If you've got some catching up to do, order your tickets now; you may have to wait a few months to get in.

■ **Southland Legacy #2:**
  Voices of the Southern Experience.

College students Down South call it "grit lit." The more serious minded of us refer to it as the literature of the "Southern Renaissance" or the "Southern genre." What everybody is talking about—and has been for decades—is the highly acclaimed literary tradition of the twentieth-century Southland. Short stories, novels, poetry, and plays—some of the best ever written—were made in Dixie, as were their creators.

Understanding the South and Southerners isn't an easy thing to do, but you can make a lot more sense of the southern experience by listening to our voices of experience. We'll even get you started with our Suggested Grit Lit Reading List. Pick yourself a theme and see what some of us have had to say for ourselves.

Coming of Age in the South: Young folk growing up in a changing South were often used as metaphors for the South's own coming of age. Read: Carson McCullers, *The Heart Is a Lonely Hunter;* Harper Lee, *To Kill a Mockingbird;* Thomas Wolfe, *Look Homeward, Angel;* Alice Walker, *The Color Purple;* T. R. Pearson, *A Short History of a Small Place;* Padgett Powell, *Edisto.*

The Decaying South: Themes of anguish and desolation, moral confusion, and social decay in the Southland. Read: Flannery O'Connor, *A Good Man Is Hard to Find and Other Short Stories;* Tennessee Williams, *A Streetcar Named Desire;* William Faulkner, *Absalom, Absalom!*

Decadence, Eccentricity, and Other Controversial Subjects: A taste of the wilder side of the Southland. Read; Erskine Caldwell, *Tobacco Road:* Tennessee Williams, *Cat on a Hot Tin Roof;* Florence King, *Southern Ladies and Gentlemen.*

Small-Town and Rural South: Recountings and re-creations of days forever gone in Dixie. Read: Eudora Welty, *The Wide Net;* Truman Capote, *Tree of Night;* Ferrol Sams, *Run with the Horseman;* Olive Ann Burns, *Cold Sassy Tree;* Fannie Flagg, *Fried Green Tomatoes at the Whistlestop Cafe;* Richard Marius, *The Coming of Rain.*

The Glorified Good-Old-Boy Life: Contemporary southern-fried ruminations by the quasi-Good Old Boy set. Read: Lewis Grizzard, *Elvis Is Dead and I Don't Feel So Good Myself;* Roy Blount, Jr., *Crackers;* William Price Fox, *Chitlin Strut and Other Madrigals;* Bo Whaley, *All I Ever Wanted Was a Piece of Cornbread and a Cadillac.*

■ **Southland Legacy #3:**
  There's No House Like the Big House

We could go on till the cows come home about all the impressive architectural accomplishments of the Southland. From the likes of George Washington and Thomas Jefferson (architects of the new American republic) to John Portman (controversial New South architect of modernist monoliths), the architectural imprints of Southerners are legion and legendary.

Houmas House was the setting of the movie, Hush Hush, Sweet Charlotte.

But without a doubt, the architecture that's nearest and dearest to our southern hearts is much closer to home, because home is where the heart is in Dixie. Just ask someone who's ever laid eyes on any of the palatial homes of the plantation South. They're deservedly the pride and joy of southern architecture.

This fancier side of southern living was born out of the glory days of farming and trading staple crops (like tobacco, indigo, rice, and cotton) when those few and fortunate folk who thusly accumulated their wealth often situated themselves in equally glorious accommodations.

Our ever-present southern sense of place has seen to it that many of these homes are still proudly standing across the Southland. So although you won't find Tara (which, as all Southerners know, never existed), you can still find plenty of resplendent mansions on view, any of which would have equally well suited Miss Scarlett and her clan.

Greek Revival plantation homes: If it's the Old South you're itching to see, you can't do better than a Greek Revival plantation mansion. Once you've seen any of these majestic manor houses, you'll know why Greek Revival style was especially trendy during the early-to-mid-nineteenth century among the Deep South's wealthiest planters. A sampling of our many standouts includes:

- *Dunleith,* Natchez, Mississippi (c. 1856, National Historic Landmark).
- *Gaineswood,* Demopolis, Alabama (1843–1861).

It was here at Oakley House that houseguest John James Audubon painted thirty-two of his celebrated "Birds of America" works.

- *Houmas House,* Burnside, Louisiana (1840, National Register of Historic Places).
- *John Thomas Grant House,* Athens, Georgia (1857–1859).
- *Sturdivant Hall,* Selma, Alabama (1853, National Register).

"Cottage" Plantation Homes: Before there was Greek Revival grandeur, there was the less formal, but still distinguished, cottage style of plantation home. In fact, cottage-style plantation houses are more native to Dixie in their design than their grandiose successors. Designed to cope with muggy and buggy coastal climates, these wood-framed homes typically were raised off the ground and featured high ceilings, many tall windows, and expansive open-air verandas across the front and back. The grandest include:

- *Rosedown,* St. Francisville, Louisiana (1835).
- *Oakley House,* St. Francisville, Louisiana (1799).
- *Fripp Plantation,* Beaufort, South Carolina (c. 1800).

"Traditional-style" Estate Homes: The founding fathers of the South's plantation and land-owning society often reinterpreted Old World architectural styles (Georgian or Palladian) for their estate homes. Theirs were the homesteads of the *real* Old South—the family seats of those settling colonists who helped found and govern the southern states—and should not be confused, as those

Berkeley Plantation, the ancestral home of two U.S. presidents, William Henry Harrison and Benjamin Harrison.

who are sticklers for accuracy will point out, with the nouveau riche palaces of first-generation antebellum planters who had only recently made good. So there.

Distinguished examples of these traditional-style ancestral homes include:

* *Berkeley Plantation,* Charles City, Virginia (1726).

* *Westover,* Charles City County, Virginia (1730–1734).
* *Drayton Hall,* Charleston County, South Carolina (1742).
* *Carnton,* Franklin, Tennessee (1826, National Historic Landmark).

Answers to "Do You Know Your Southern Celebrities' Claims to Fame" Quiz on page 92.
1. Actor DeForrest Kelley. 2. Actress Louise Fletcher. 3. Actor Jim Varney. 4. Actor Henry Gibson. 5. Actor George Hamilton.

CELEBRITY SONS AND DAUGHTERS

The Dixie roll call of giants among men and women is so long you would be late for your own funeral if you listened to it all. That's because Southerners were making a name for themselves even before the United States had a name of its own (if you think this sounds a little bigheaded, talk to a Virginian).

Remember, we Southerners are taught early on that we're supposed to amount to something (heaven help you if you're a low-down, good-for-nothing lazy sack of bones; you should know better), so no wonder so many of us have done just that. No wonder the list keeps getting longer every day.

To prove that we're anything but all talk and no action, we're naming names (Sports heroes get their own list in chapter 8). They belong to the homefolk of today who've made a name for themselves and, in the spirit of fairness, a few whose names are mud.

■ Famous Faces

They look as familiar as the back of your hand, but did you know they were born Down South?

Claude Akins—Nelson, Georgia
Kim Basinger—Athens, Georgia
Kathy Bates—Memphis
Ned Beatty—Louisville
Warren Beatty—Richmond
David Brinkley—Wilmington, North Carolina
Helen Gurley Brown—Green Forest, Arkansas
Nell Carter—Birmingham
William Conrad—Louisville
Howard Cosell—Winston-Salem, North Carolina
Johnny Depp—Owensboro, Kentucky
Lawrence Fishburne—Augusta, Georgia
Fannie Flagg—Birmingham
Louise Fletcher—Birmingham
Morgan Freeman—Memphis
Henry Gibson—Fairhope, Alabama
Andy Griffith—Mount Airy, North Carolina
Bryant Gumbel—New Orleans
George Hamilton—Memphis
Tess Harper—Mammoth Springs, Arkansas
Kitty Carlisle Hart—New Orleans
Jan Hooks—Decatur, Georgia
Holly Hunter—Conyers, Georgia
Kate Jackson—Birmingham
James Earl Jones—Tate County, Mississippi
Stacey Keach—Savannah
DeForrest Kelley—Atlanta
Dorothy Lamour—New Orleans
John Larroquette—New Orleans
Spike Lee—Atlanta
Rob Lowe—Charlottesville, Virginia
Andie MacDowell—Gaffney, South Carolina
Shirley MacLaine—Richmond
Gerald McRaney—Collins, Mississippi
Ben Murphy—Jonesboro, Arkansas
Patricia Neal—Packard, Kentucky
Bert Parks—Atlanta

DO YOU KNOW YOUR SOUTHERN CELEBRITIES' CLAIMS TO FAME?

1. He's best known as "Bones," the physician of *Star Trek* fame.
2. She gave a bone-chilling performance as the evil Nurse Ratched in *One Flew Over the Cuckoo's Nest.*
3. Everybody knows him as Ernest, Vern's friend.
4. This former "Laugh-in" star was a country music singer in Robert Altman's film *Nashville.*
5. He's as famous for his suntan as any of his movie roles.

Answers on page 90.

Annie Potts—Nashville
Burt Reynolds—Waycross, Georgia
Eric Roberts—Biloxi, Mississippi
Julia Roberts—Smyrna, Georgia
Nipsey Russell—Atlanta
Diane Sawyer—Glasgow, Kentucky
George C. Scott—Wise, Virginia
Cybill Shepherd—Memphis
Richard Simmons—New Orleans
Mary Steenburgen—Little Rock
Stella Stevens—Yazoo City, Mississippi
Fran Tarkenton—Richmond
Jim Varney—Lexington
Vanna White—Myrtle Beach, South Carolina
Demond Wilson—Valdosta, Georgia
Oprah Winfrey—Kosciusko, Mississippi
Joanne Woodward—Thomasville, Georgia

■ **Music Makers**

You're sure to know their music, but did you know from whence they came in Dixie?

Alabama: Nat King Cole. Emmylou Harris. Jim Nabors. Lionel Ritchie. Toni Tenille. Tammy Wynette. Country music band Alabama.

Arkansas: Glen Campbell. Johnny Cash. Al Green. K. T. Oslin. Charlie Rich.

Georgia: Ray Charles. Gladys Knight. Jessye Norman. Little Richard. Jerry Reed. Trisha Yearwood. Pop/Rock bands REM and The B-52's.

Kentucky: Rosemary Clooney. Billy Ray Cyrus. Don Everly. Crystal Gayle. Tom T. Hall. Naomi and Wynonna Judd. Bill Monroe. Mary Travers.

Louisiana: Louis Armstrong. Van Cliburn. Harry Connick, Jr. Fats Domino. Al Hirt. Mahalia Jackson.

Jerry Lee Lewis. Branford and Wynton Marsalis. Jelly Roll Morton. Hank Williams, Jr.

Mississippi: Jimmy Buffett. Jerry Clower. Bo Diddley. W. C. Handy. B. B. King. Elvis Presley. Leontyne Price. Charlie Pride. Jimmie Rodgers. Conway Twitty. Muddy Waters.

North Carolina: Crash Craddock. Donna Fargo. Roberta Flack. Ronnie Milsap. Thelonious Monk. Earl Scruggs. Randy Travis. Doc Watson.

South Carolina: Chubby Checker. Dizzy Gillespie. Eartha Kitt.

Tennessee: Roy Acuff. Greg Allman. Chet Atkins. James Brown. Rita Coolidge. Lester Flatt. Aretha Franklin. Tennessee Ernie Ford. Amy Grant. Isaac Hayes. Loretta Lynn. Dolly Parton. Minnie Pearl. Bessie Smith. Tina Turner. Kitty Wells.

Virginia: Pearl Bailey. The Carter Family. June Carter Cash. Roy Clark. Patsy Cline. Ella Fitzgerald. Wayne Newton. Kate Smith.

■ Trail Blazers and Trendsetters

They're some of today's biggest thinkers, and they're from the South. Even if you don't recognize all their names, we bet you'll recognize how they made a name for themselves.

James Earl ("Jimmy") Carter (Plains, Georgia): Former peanut farmer, Georgia governor, and thirty-ninth president of the United States. He was most admired for his foreign policy achievements and humanitarian efforts, but his political downfall was caused by inflation and Iran's spiritual leader, the Ayatollah Khomeni.

Bill Clinton (Hope, Arkansas): Baby Boomer, Rhodes scholar, former governor of Arkansas and forty-second president of the United States, he'll have his hands full as he leads the nation toward the next century.

Elizabeth Hanford Dole (Salisbury, North Carolina): Head of American Red Cross, former U.S. secretary of transportation under President Ronald Reagan, former Federal Trade Commission chief, and wife of Senator Bob Dole, she's a *magna cum laude* graduate of the iron-hand-in-velvet-glove school for southern ladies.

Billy Graham (Charlotte, North Carolina): World-famous television evangelist and religious leader; he doesn't need his own cable television network to spread the gospel.

Charlayne Hunter-Gault (Due West, South Carolina): First black woman student at University of Georgia; now an award-winning (two Emmys and a Peabody) journalist and correspondent for public television's McNeil/Lehrer News-Hour.

Jesse Jackson (Greenville, South Carolina): Civil rights pioneer and leader; director of Operation Breadbasket; founder and president of the Rainbow Coalition, his track record is as imposing as his oratory.

Alexander Julian (Chapel Hill, North Carolina): Clothing designer acclaimed for his Colours line; known for his distinctive tailored stylings using subtle colorations and textures.

Charles Kuralt (Wilmington, North Carolina): CBS news correspondent for the Emmy award-winning program "On the Road," he's the gifted chronicler of American life and culture.

Bob Pittman (Forest Hill, Mississippi): Visionary of cable TV's Music Television at age twenty-seven, he now heads the successful MTV Networks (MTV, Nickelodeon, VH-1).

Fred Smith (Memphis): Unfazed when his Yale professor considered the idea C-grade, he followed his hunch to found the first and largest overnight delivery service, Federal Express.

Isaac Tigrett (Memphis): Founder of the trendy and successful Hard Rock Cafe enterprise (called the "Smithsonian of Rock and Roll" by actor Dan Aykroyd).

Ted Turner III (transplanted Georgian): Controversial media scion (Turner Broadcasting system), brash sports mogul (Atlanta Braves and Hawks), daredevil yachtsman (America's Cup winner, 1977), and self-acknowledged braggadocio.

Andrew Young (New Orleans): Civil Rights leader, Georgia politician, and former U.S. ambassador to the United Nations.

■ **Rogue's Gallery**

And then there are our skeletons in the closet, those Southerners whose reputations have gotten a little tarnished amongst the homefolk of Dixie. Some hands-down winners of this generation's Your Name Is Mud award include:

John and Rita Jenrette (South Carolina). This former U.S. senator was caught with his hand in the ABSCAM cookie jar in 1980 to the tune of 50,000 cookies. His siren wife, Rita, didn't exactly paint a picture of clean living to a lot of Southerners, either, when she bared more than her soul for *Playboy* after John's conviction.

Bert Lance (Georgia). Lance has the dubious distinction of being one of the South's most famous has-beens. Exposed for such mischief as check kiting and shady loan making, T. Bertram Lance found himself making many exits, including his role as U.S. budget director and chairman of Walter Mondale's presidential campaign, Georgia's Democratic party, and the Calhoun (Georgia) First National Bank.

Jim and Tammy Bakker. They're not Southerners by birth, but since they were happy to situate their "gospel of prosperity" empire and their Babylonian lifestyle in Dixie, we figure they deserve the Rogue's Gallery. In a land where enough is considered plenty, it was bad form for Jim and Tammy to flaunt their worldly ways. It was even worse that they funded their pleasures from the offering plate. But where they *really* went astray in the eyes of most Southerners was entertaining the world at the expense of God *and* the Southland, holy subjects indeed to desecrate around these parts.

BIG BUCKS IN DIXIE: WHO'S MADE 'EM

Don't let that humble I'm-just-a-hard-workin'-southern-boy demeanor fool you. Behind that plainly dressed, courteous facade might be a Southerner so rich he could buy half the state if he wanted. There are plenty of such Southerners around, whether they subscribe to the traditional southern approach ("Be modest") or find the New South style ("A little flash don't mean trash") more to their liking.

Some of our homefolk roll in so much money that the rest of the nation (and sometimes, the world) has taken notice, including *Forbes* magazine's list of Wealthiest Americans and other such dynastic barometers.

Now that's what's known as living high on the hog—by anybody's standards—and here are more than forty such southern names who qualify, stock market gyrations notwithstanding.

■ Billionaires

Heirs of Samuel M. Walton, Bentonville, Arkansas: Until his death in 1992, he was the richest man in the United States, and he and his brother got that way by building their superlatively successful chain of Wal-Mart stores with retailing smarts and unpretentious style. His widow and children share assets with an estimated worth of more than $25 billion.

Forrest E. Mars, Jr., and John F. Mars, McLean and Arlington, Virginia: Heirs to their dad's candy empire, the sons of Mars continue the family tradition of satisfying sweet teeth the world over. (Forrest Mars, Sr., is semi-retired and lives in Las Vegas.) Dad and heirs' worth is placed at more than $9 billion.

Anne Cox Chambers, Atlanta: She was ambassador to Belgium during the Carter administration and, with her sister, shares the wealth of media conglomerate Cox Enterprises (built by their dad). The two ladies control a company worth well over $4 billion.

Robert E. ("Ted") Turner III, Roswell, Georgia: Young Ted erected a fortune from an ailing family billboard business, which became a springboard for even more visible accomplishments: cable television, professional sports teams (Atlanta Braves and Hawks), yachting, and movies. Net worth: nearly $2 billion.

James L. Walton, Bentonville, Arkansas: Brother of Sam, his own share of the Wal-Mart fortune stands today at more than $1.25 billion.

Jackson T. Stephens and family, Little Rock: With his late brother Witt, he built a billion-dollar net worth from investment banking (including stock offerings for buddy Sam Walton), plus lucrative gas and oil holdings.

The Brown Family of Louisville: For more than a century, this family has made its name and money in distilling (Old Forester, Jack Daniel's, Southern Comfort) and, recently, fine china (Lenox, Dansk). Together, the Browns' worth is in the neighborhood of $1 billion.

John T. Lupton, Chattanooga, Tennessee, and Elizabeth Lupton Davenport, Lookout Mountain, Tennessee: Coca-Cola has been the Real Thing for the Luptons ever since granddad became a bottler 100 years ago. The family cola domain had expanded to a large chunk of the West and Southwest before these two heirs sold the dynasty back to Daddy Coke in the eighties—for a chunk of change worth about a billion bucks today.

Paul Mellon, Upperville, Virginia: Heir to his grandfather's banking wealth and social clout. Philanthropist and world-renowned art collector, his net worth is at $1 billion.

■ **$500 Million to $1 Billion**

Winthrop P. Rockefeller, Winrock Farm, Arkansas: He's an heir to the J. D. Rockefeller family fortune, son of a two-time former Arkansas governor, and is involved in banking and charitable causes.

Jack Kent Cooke, Middleburg, Virginia: This former Canadian made it rich in radio, newspaper, and magazines, then used the proceeds to buy (and sell) professional sports franchises, cable TV systems, and prime real estate.

Roger Milliken, Spartanburg, South Carolina: He's at the helm of a profitable 120-year-old family tradition in textiles. There's added wealth in his extensive stock holdings of a retail store group.

Donald J. and Barbara Tyson, Springdale and Fayetteville, Arkansas: Any way you cut it, theirs is the nation's leading poultry supplier, having laid a golden egg by selling chickens and prepared foods to grocers and restaurants.

The Turner Family, Columbus, Georgia: Granddad W. C. Bradley wisely invested in Coca-Cola early on, then continued to line the family vault with stakes in sports apparel, barbecue grills, and smart investments.

John M. Harbert III, Birmingham: A self-made millionaire whose fortune was, literally, built through construction ventures. Stock investments help to further fill the Harbert coffers.

The Richardson Family of Greensboro, North Carolina (and elsewhere): A pharmaceutical success story was born with the concoction of Vicks Vaporub in 1907; so was a family fortune, from this and other medicine cabinet products.

Bernard Marcus and Arthur Blank, Atlanta: Their self-made fortunes keep building, thanks to their booming Home Depot chain of hardware and building supply stores.

Floyd D. Gottwald, Jr., and Bruce Gottwald, Richmond: Savvy business investing (and divesting) in manufac-?turing (paper, gasoline additives, plastics, metals, pharmaceuticals) and insurance paid off in handsome yields.

John D. Hollingsworth, Greenville, South Carolina: His mechanical know-how in the textile industry spun him a heavy net worth, as did savvy real estate investing.

E. Bronson Ingram, Nashville: He parlayed family inheritances into a gargantuan enterprise of book and video distribution.

The Murphy Family, El Dorado, Arkansas: Charles, Jr., followed in his father's oil patch footsteps to engineer a lucrative and diversified energy corporation; now he shares the helm with siblings and in-laws.

The Belk Family, Charlotte: This century-old retailing enterprise remains largely in the hands of descendants of founder William Belk. At last count, they held close to 300 stores in Dixie.

Frank Batten, Virginia Beach: His uncle's newspaper was the springboard to a publishing, broadcasting, and cable TV empire.

■ $250 Million to $500 Million

Thomas J. Frist, Jr., and family, Nashville: His Hospital Corporation of America has worked miracles among an industry formerly suffering from chronic financial ill-health.

The Russell Family, Alexander City, Alabama: They've clad America in leisure togs and athletic uniforms, including a sizable number of college and major league teams.

The Close Family, Fort Mill, South Carolina: They share in the generous wealth woven from Springmaid bed linens and prudent reinvesting.

Constance Simons du Pont Darden, Norfolk, Virginia, and Eleanor Francis du Pont Rust, Thomasville, Georgia: Their family's extensive financial dynasty has situated these heiresses with sizable shares of investment holdings.

The Bingham Family, Louisville: Patriarch Barry Bingham carried on his dad's publishing tradition and later expanded into broadcasting. Highly publicized squabbles amongst his heirs compelled him to sell out in the late eighties and divide the ample spoils.

C. D. ("Dick") Spangler, Jr., Chapel Hill: He helped fix his dad's ailing bank and later sold it to NCNB, then further fattened his wallet with investments in North Carolina companies.

R. Randal and Gary W. Rollins, Atlanta: Heirs of commerce scion Orville W. Rollins, they share his wealth from pest control, security systems, and oil and gas enterprises.

Leon Levine, Charlotte: In less than thirty years, Leon Levine amassed big-time money from small-town shoppers with his Family Dollar Stores, now a familiar sight in almost half the United States.

J. B. Hunt, Springdale, Arkansas: Yet another boy from the Ozarks who struck the mother lode, J. B. made his first strike in the poultry supply business and a lucrative second with truck and trailer transport.

Jesse ("Mack") Robinson, Atlanta: This financier banked his future upon banking and prospered in the process. He's furthered his fortune by bankrolling other business ventures.

James McGlothlin and family, Bristol, Tennessee: Smart moves in coal mining paid his way for profitable forays into oil, gas, real estate.

Robert C. Goizueta, Atlanta: This first-generation Cuban-American has been at the helm of Coca-Cola since 1981 and is well paid for his success at waking a once-sleepwalking giant.

Claude B. Pennington, Baton Rouge: He made his money through oil and gas (drilling, leases, etc.) and likes to give generously to Louisiana State University.

J. R. Hyde III, Memphis: He furthered his granddad's fortune in grocery wholesaling with food and pharmacy retailing, then dramatically drove up his net worth with a chain of auto supply stores.

John Brooks Fuqua, Atlanta: He's a wheeling-'n'-dealing mogul whose entrepreneurial savvy amassed him a massive portfolio of wealth. His smarts in commerce and a $10 million donation accorded him the honor of namesake of Duke's business school.

James Lee Clayton, Knoxville, Tennessee: Poor country boy done good, via manufacture of mobile homes—*lots.*

■ **Those of Untold Wealth**

They also live high on the hog—but how high, we can't be sure.

The Belz Family, Memphis: Long-time buyers and developers of real estate in Tennessee and now points elsewhere, they keep things in the family and to themselves.

Frederick W. Smith, Memphis: He staked his family bus-line inheritance on a lofty idea and won, successfully building an overnight air express business and sparking an entirely new industry.

Angelo J. Bruno and family, Birmingham: Their grocery super-stores are where Deep South shoppers go to fill their pantries.

Marion Day Smith, Atlanta: Her husband built a fortune by building the Day's Inn budget hotel chain.

James F. Harrison, Chattanooga: He slaked his thirst for fortune with immense holdings in Coca-Cola bottling operations.

Raymond L. Danner, Nashville: He fattened the family bank accounts by feeding lots of hungry Southerners in his Shoney's restaurants.

Arthur L. Williams, Jr., Monroe, Georgia: Demonstrating that investing in futures doesn't have to mean speculating on pork bellies, he built a nationally respected insurance empire.

William S. Farish III, Versailles, Kentucky: Heir to the Humble Oil fortune (and so forth), he's a devoted member of the Kentucky horse set (breeding, racing, polo).

Winton M. Blount, Montgomery, Alabama: Thinking big was his ticket to grand-scale construction projects the world over and even a businessman's overhaul of the U.S. postal system during the 1980s.

CHAPTER FIVE

Social Studies, Southern Style

Required Reading for Navigating the Social Ropes Down South

Every Southerner has a sense of place, but some enjoy a more elevated sense of place than others. These are the Southlanders who, as we like to put it, live high on the hog. They walk in tall cotton. They live off the fat of the land because they're the ones with the prime acreage. They're the ones who belong to southern society, as in the high variety.

Southern Style for these folks is a whole 'nother ball of wax. On top of the privileges granted by being born and bred in Dixie, they possess the perquisites that can only come from being born and bred to the right social station.

Life in the upper reaches of the Southland's social strata comes with its own rules and regulations. Like everything else that has to do with Southern Style, it is steeped in tradition and of our own creation. So if you want to understand what it's like to walk on the high side of life Down South, you'd do well to sit tight and read on.

KNOWING YOUR PLACE IN SOUTHLAND SOCIETY

Every Southerner occupies a rung on the ladder of southern society and, as the saying goes, we know our place. Your place is assigned at birth, and you die in the same place you started. No matter what happens in between, Southlanders know you can't change your place in Dixie. Your place is your lifelong social station—the Down-South version of AKC registration.

Your place is assigned according to the rules of southern society. The rules are very old. The rules do not change. The rules are what put you in your place and keep you there. The rules are why some people Not From Here have used such words as "provincial" and "unfathomable" to describe the southern social order.

The rules are yet another example of why Southerners say to this day, "There are just some things about the South that you can't explain to Yankees." These are the rules:

■ **Rule #1: An approved southern pedigree is what determines your social station in Dixie.**

Don't think twice about getting in the southern social register if you don't have a reputable family name from an old southern family. What really counts is who your mama and daddy are and who their mamas and daddies were and how they earned their distinguished family names.

■ **Rule #2: If you come from old southern money and an old southern family, you're really sitting pretty.**

We must admit, a lot of folks in the upper reaches of southern society have more in common than a good family name, and that's a good net worth, probably several generations' worth on *both* sides of the family. This is indeed fortunate since a lifestyle suitable to such a place on the social ladder Down South takes as much discretionary income as it does proper discretion (more on this shortly). So while a good name is indeed rather to be had than great riches in Dixie, most Southerners in the Order take a liking to having both.

However, if you're of "reduced circumstances" in Dixie (translated: your family lost its wealth during Reconstruction or due to some other unfortunate cause), you haven't lost your place. You'll always have a place in southern society; for as long as your honorable name is intact in the Southland, so also is your good social station—even if you *are* wearing the same ball gown for the third year in a row.

■ **Rule #3: If you don't already have a place in the Order, don't count on getting one.**

Your elevated place is inherited and passed on; rarely is it acquired (the notable exception being the posses-

100

sion of an M.D. degree). This applies even to those who "marry up," since everyone in town will be quite aware of your more humble origins. The moral of this rule is: It's a sight easier to improve your address than your social station in Dixie.

■ **Rule #4: Don't confuse social station with social status in the South.**

Merciful heaven, social status is something to be strived for, not born with, or, worse yet, displayed. Social status is a reward for social climbing, a pursuit that may get you the attention of other limelighters but won't move you up one skinny rung as far as your social station in Dixie is concerned.

DO YOU SIT IN HIGH PLACES IN DIXIE?

If you were born with a place on the highest social rungs of all, you belong to the order of the Old Southern Family, the most desirable pedigree of all to have (or wish you had). A place in the Order means that you come from what we Southerners call an "established southern family" or "a long line of really fine folk."

It means your family has been a part of the southern landscape for many generations and probably had a hand in putting your county on the map way back when. It means your people are some of the most upstanding, outstanding, and longstanding Southerners around. When you're an Orderly, most everybody around your part of the state knows your family—or knows of it—and thinks well of it.

Should you belong to the Order, you already know there's a place permanently saved for you in Dixie society. In fact, you *are* Dixie society, the old-line, good-name variety, which is as high on the ladder as anyone can get down here. Should you wonder if you belong, well, you probably don't. But just in case, take our quiz below.

■ **Qualification Quiz**

It's a safe bet that you belong to the Order of the Old Southern Family if you can answer yes to most of the following:

1. Your family has been in the same county for more than five generations.
2. Your family owns property in the country.
3. At least one of your ancestors was an officer in the War.
4. At least one street or building in your hometown bears a family name.
5. Your mama was a Junior Leaguer (or the like) in your town.

6. Your daddy is/was a deacon or elder in the church.
7. One of the men in your family was a judge or an elected official.
8. There's a scholarship or endowment in the family name at one of the state colleges.

If you answer yes to all or most of the following, you don't have a piddling chance of belonging to the Order.

1. Your parents moved to town from Michigan when the mill opened in '54.
2. Your house has a satellite dish in the yard.
3. At least one of your ancestors was a Bluecoat in the War.
4. The only street in town that bears your family name is the one with your mailbox.
5. Your mama had to work outside the home.
6. Your daddy rarely ever darkens the door of the church.
7. One of the men in your family served time.
8. It's a family tradition to attend the local technical school.

SOUTHERN STYLE #4: THE ORDERLIES
Born to the Order with mint julep cups in their hands.

Geoffrey Beene
Grey Flannel cologne

18K gold and lapis cuff
links (gift from wife on
10th wedding anniversary)

Gold and onyx studs

Cartier tank watch

Ralph Lauren tuxedo

Highlighted hair
(gracefully disguises the gray)

Clip-on 18K gold cuff earrings

Chanel No. 22 perfume

18K Piaget watch with
diamond bezel and bracelet
Judith Leiber enameled
seashell clutch

1.5 carat emerald dinner ring
on right hand (grandmother's),
1.3 carat diamond and
sapphire wedding band guard
on left

Off-the-shoulder creation by
Arnold Scaasi (mature, yet
festive, design)

HIM

HER

Name: James Travis Thurston IV (goes by
   Travis)
Profession: Managing Partner at the city's
   oldest law firm
Education: McCallie School, Chattanooga BA,
   Washington & Lee, '58; JD, University of
   Mississippi, '61
Drives: BMW 733i around town, Jeep
   Wagoneer to lake house or duck hunting
Social Resume: Member of old-line country
club (President of Board,'78) and yacht club at
lake
   Chair, Endowment Committee, Children's
Hospital
   Founder's Circle, W & L
   Distinguished Alumni, University of
Mississippi Law School
   Member, Republican National Committee
   Church (Episcopal) steering committee
   Ducks Unlimited
*Last Book Read: Whistling Dixie, Dispatches
   from the South* by John Shelton Reed
Overheard saying: "I don't believe I know his
   people."

Name: Mary Maude (*nee* Markham) Thurston
   (goes by Mary Maude)
Profession: Fundraiser and patron of socially
   correct causes, mother of three grown
children
Education: Harpeth Hall (Nashville), '56
   BFA, University of Mississippi, '60
Drives: Mercedes Benz 400
Social Resume: President, Friends of
Children's Hospital
   Board of Directors, Art Museum
   Former Chair, state chapter of Historic Trust
for Preservation
   Sustaining member, Junior League
Board, '72–'76, KAθ Alumni
   Chair, Symphony Ball, '88, '89.
   . . . plus more than 30 years of endless key
   positions on various committees, special
   events, and advisory boards as befits a lady
   born to the Order.
Last Book Read: Colony, by Anne Rivers
   Siddons
Overhead Saying: "It's in the genes, dear."

103

TOEING THE LINE IN SOUTHERN SOCIETY

As representatives of the Order of Old Southern Families, you have to toe the line when it comes to carrying off your special kind of Southern Style. You may secretly hanker to spend your Saturday nights at the Talladega race track or wish you knew how to make ceramic bookends, but if you walk in tall cotton in Dixie, you know better than to let loose those fantasies, even to your own mother.

Why, that wouldn't become your social station a'tall; you *know* folks would think you'd gone plumb out of your *mind* and your family would surely be shamed to *death* when the rest of the town heard about it, which they most certainly would.

No, ma'am, the higher your rung on the social ladder, the more carefully you had better tread. Conformity is one of the essential ground rules of an elevated social station Down South. Sticking out like a sore thumb is not. And since the consequences of not toeing the line are losing face or, worst of all, losing place, 99 percent of those in the Order choose to behave themselves as becomes their station.

Don't think, however, that toeing the line is too heavy a burden for these Southerners. Truth is, most folk in Dixie would give their eye teeth to have such a row to hoe. Just consider the sorts of accommodations you'd have to make to suit your station in tall cotton:

■ **Twenty-five Ways to Grace Your Place in Southern Society**

1. Wear traditional, conservative, and expensive clothes. Men should favor the preppy/Ralph Lauren look; women should be partial to the "grown up little girl" look (Laura Ashley, Belle France, Eagle's Eye, etc.) whenever possible.

2. Live in established, traditional neighborhoods in spacious, traditional-looking residences with classic, traditional interiors. The older the neighborhood and your home's architectural style, the better. Young marrieds may start out in a newer, more suburban home but later will move to one of the prestige addresses.

3. Enroll your children in the same private schools that you and your tended.

4. Belong to the country club and perhaps a town club; belong to civic and political organizations. Wives should belong to the Junior League or comparable ladies' auxiliary. Patronize the fine arts or performing arts; be active in your college and Greek alumni organizations.

5. Build a lake house or, better yet, a beach house. Best of all, spruce up the one you inherited from your mother's side of the family. Move the family there each summer (Dad comes to visit on weekends).

6. Have portraits painted of the children (and maybe the dog) when they're young. Have yours and your spouse's done before your fortieth birthdays.

7. Give substantial sums of money to the church building fund.

8. Renovate the family ancestral home (or an old, in-town home) for your own family to live in. Open it for annual home tours.

9. Send your kids to summer camp in the North Carolina mountains for a month.

10. Leave hubby at home and go to New York each fall for a three-day shopping spree and museum circuit with a pal from the hospital auxiliary. Take your daughters along, too, and stay on the Junior League floor at the Plaza.

11. While the wife is in New York, join your duck-hunting cohorts in Stuttgart, Arkansas, for a fall weekend of men, guns, ducks, dogs, and whiskey.

12. Send your daughter to a good southern girls' school for her first two years in college and then let her transfer to the state university so she can pledge a sorority and find a husband.

13. Take the family skiing in Crested Butte, Montana, each year over Thanksgiving.

14. Introduce your college-age daughter to society with her debut. Spend a small fortune and a year of the family's time for the clothes, the parties, the ball, and the requisite community service work.

15. Invest in southern primitive folk art. Scout the rural areas for the next Mattie Lou O'Kelley or the Reverend Howard Finster. Invest in prints and sculpture commemorating the War Between the States.

16. Bankroll your college-junior son while he and a classmate backpack across Europe one summer.

17. Spend your fall and winter weekends fox hunting, tending your horses, and hobnobbing with your horsey-set friends.

18. Where applicable, bankroll your son's and daughter's participation(s) in the courts of Mardi Gras, first as children and later as young adults.

19. Donate a family heirloom to the area art museum.

20. Open an antique linens store in a renovated store-front building, using a $50,000 "loan" from your husband.

21. Leave the wives at home and take a few of your pals deep-sea fishing on your fifty-foot Bertram for a week each summer.

22. Visit the Holy Land with your spouse on a church-sponsored tour led by the pastor.

23. Invest heavily in the breeding and training of championship bird dogs with hopes for qualifying them for the National Field Trial Competition in Grand Junction, Tennessee

24. Purchase a limited-partnership interest in a Thoroughbred horse racing syndicate with hopes of having your own Seattle Slew success story.

25. Spend large sums of money and time becoming a two-goal polo player, tending your ponies, and traveling to and from meets with your club.

OLD SOCIETY AND THE NEW SOUTH

Who'd have ever thought they'd live to see the day when some of the unwritten laws of old southern society would be regularly bent, even by many of Dixie's most socially astute constituents? Surely great-grandmother Cunningham never expected that what she considered *faux pas* would become *status quo,* but, then again, did great-grandmother Cunningham ever expect life without corsets?

Lordy, Lordy, what *is* the South coming to?

Welcome to the New South. One hundred years after Georgian Henry Grady made his "New South" appeal to Northern financiers, there really is a New South everywhere you look in Dixie. And that includes some of our most southern social conventions.

For those of you in the Order, this means the advent of the Old Society/New South lifestyle—living in the time-honored manner of old southern society (some things never change), but doing so with a New South twist. Translated, this means respect the old traditions but don't be an old fogey about them, either. Here's how to do it.

■ Let the twain meet—and mix.

Don't be a bit surprised to see old money and new money rubbing elbows at even the swankiest social clubs and functions in Dixie. Let's be pragmatic; it's new money (and there's lots and lots of it being made) that is helping to rev up southern commerce and culture. Those folks may not be from one of our older families, dear, but some of them *are* so *interesting* to talk to, don't you think?

■ Be modest—in a Mercedes.

No longer do you need to eschew the glitz or save for such glittering occasions as merger weddings or debutante balls (when it gets toted out in full tilt). In this day of the New South, it's quite all right to look luxe, even when you're slumming.

So go right ahead and get that $75,000 BMW and wear that $10,000 Piaget watch. The accoutrements of worldly high style no longer automatically label you as flashy trash in Dixie. Just be sure not to act pretentious, though, because not even in this era of the New South can we tolerate social self-promotion.

■ Downhome has gone uptown.

Being cosmopolitan in the metropolitan South has become the preferred mode for many Southerners. In these meccas of the New South, "supper" has become "dinner" and "eating dinner" has become "doing lunch." Parking-lot fund raisers are now referred to as "*al fresco* benefits." Folks sit in sunrooms, not on front porches, and knock on the front door (expected, of course), not on the back door (drop-in, naturally).

In these uptown environs, it's even OK to talk about power and money— who has it and how they got it—since those are the rewards of the urban harvest. What's not OK is for you to forget your genteel upbringing while growing those greenbacks. Lose your manners and you'll lose your "in" with southern society, even in the starry-eyed New South. Some things *never* change in Dixie.

THE JUNIOR LEAGUE: SENIOR SOCIAL STATEMENT

You'll find one in most of the South's larger cities; sometimes two or more. There are about fifty of them in the Southland, including the largest in the world. You'll have to pass a tough social muster to join their genteel ranks, but you'll also have to work off your derriere to remain in their good standing.

Welcome to the Junior League, ladies.

Few other volunteer organizations, if any, carry such social cachet in the Southland as its Leagues. Even in this age of the New South, League membership rosters tend to read like the local social register, and most southern ladies tend to view League membership as an infallible test of so-cial substance. Like joining a sorority as a college coed, joining the League is a natural rite of passage for southern ladies in the Order. It comes with the territory.

Detractors like to classify Leaguers as syrupy-spoken society matrons whose idea of supporting charity is to publish cute cookbooks. In truth, few volunteer organizations in Dixie can compare with the League when it comes to sheer grit, determination, and magnitude of civic service—even if its members *were* born with a silver demitasse spoon in their mouths. And besides, the vast sums of money that those cute cookbooks have ginned up for charity are anything but small potatoes.

BOWING TO SOCIETY IN THE SOUTHLAND

For most young ladies in Dixie, being crowned beauty queen or homecoming queen would be the utmost honor to receive (looking pretty and pleasing people remains an unyielding aspiration for southern women and girls). But for young ladies whose families constitute the *crème de la crème* of southern society, aspiring to such public spectacle is an unnecessary and, well, rather *undignified* pursuit. Who needs to walk a runway with nineteen other eager hopefuls in the school auditorium or shiver in the middle of a football field during halftime, when they've got something ahead of them that's much more exclusive and carries much more social panache?

Not these gals, because they get to make their debut to society. Out of all the coeds in the city, they are the ones who get to curtsy in the country club or landmark location before an appreciative gallery of the city's finest folk. They get to be feted at dozens of natty luncheons, cocktail parties, and dinners for an entire season. They might even take a year off from college to do it, and they get there without having to perform a "talent" or beam a 100-watt smile. They've got the right pedigree, and that's what matters.

So for these lasses, having such high-rolling social triumphs to anticipate does tend to make public displays of pulchritude and charm seem a shade trifling. Gracious, there's much more at stake here than a full-page picture in a yearbook; we're talking the preservation of a long-established social tradition and, really, the veneration of front-row southern society itself. Now *that's* something to take seriously.

■ The Lowdown on Coming out Down South

Tips for making sense of a southern tradition.

Making the cut: There are more coming-outs in the Southland than you can shake a long-stemmed rose at. Almost every southern city of appreciable size annually honors the daughters of its most prominent families. But the toniest debutante presentations occur in the larger cities, where the standards for qualification are loftier (sometimes *so* much so that the largest cities often have two or three debutante clubs, one for the Old Money and others for the New Money).

If your family has real social clout in your area, you'll make your debut at a major deb ball whether you hail from a small town or not. If you belong to a *really* heavy-hitting family, you could be presented twice in the same season, either in another city (probably one of your parents' hometowns) or, in some cases, in a statewide or regional presentation (and maybe even a New York City deb ball, if your family is one of Dixie's most top-hat).

108

Camellia Ball, Mobile, Alabama

When the admission qualifications get bent: In this age of the New South, even the firmly fixed admission qualifications can, on rare occasions, be waived. This happens when what we'll call the VIP Clause is invoked, which amounts to including in the debutante lineup the daughter of someone who is not a native of that city (and maybe not even the South) but is very important to the city. Look at it this way. Would *you* snub the daughter of the president of the company that brought millions and millions of dollars to your local economy and its family-owned businesses?

Fun and fund-raising: In many southern cities, the deb ball doubles as a charity benefit. Proceeds from the gala are donated to a pet cause, and often the debutantes in these clubs spend many hours in volunteer work. But elsewhere in Dixie, deb assemblies forego the higher ideals, preferring to keep the event a purely social ritual.

Pretty is as pretty does? Outside observers are invariably disappointed to discover that few of a given year's clutch of debutantes are, shall we say, raving beauties. In all fairness, we must admit that some of those faces peering out from the Sunday social page can be a little on the plain side. But lest you forget, these young ladies were not selected on the basis of such an ephemeral qualification as good looks. Nope, it's the family that counts. Not the face.

If you're curious to find out more about debutante phenomena in Dixie, you're probably not going to get too far. The reason for this is very simple: You'd already know all the skinny if you belonged to the right families. You can, however, follow next year's goings-on in your local society column ("Dr. and Mrs. Hubert Crenshaw of Lakeside Manor entertained debutantes CAROLINE WINN and KATHY CLARKE last Sunday with a brunch in the garden gazebo . . ."). And who knows, if you play your cards right, maybe you can finagle yourself an invitation to the presentation and see southern society in one of its finest hours.

■ **Noteworthy Dixie Debutante Balls**

Atlanta
    The Harvest Ball. Friday after Thanksgiving; since 1911. Old-line Atlanta all the way.
    The Phoenix Ball. The week before Christmas; since 1964.

Birmingham
    The Beaux Arts Ball. Held in February. The Magic City's old-name deb ball.
    The Christmas Ball. Held the Saturday before Christmas at the Country Club of Birmingham; since 1907.

Charleston
    St. Cecilia Ball. Held in late January; since 1762. One of the most aristocratic presentations anywhere but also the least publicized—intentionally so.

Chattanooga
    The Cotton Ball. Held in early August; since 1933. Many Cotton Ball debs are from nearby states. Highlight is a coronation of an honest-to-goodness king and queen.

Columbia, South Carolina
    The Assembly Ball. Held the weekend before Christmas; since 1889.

Durham, North Carolina
    The Debutante Cotillion and Christmas Ball. Held in late December; since 1955. For young ladies in the Durham and Chapel Hill area. Nonalcoholic.

Greenville, Mississippi
    The Delta Debutante Ball. Held in late December; since 1942. For daughters of families in the Mississippi, Arkansas, and Louisiana Delta region.

Jackson, Mississippi
    The Debutante Ball. Held the Friday night after Thanksgiving.

Lexington
    Bluegrass Charity Ball. Observed in December; since 1937.

Little Rock
    The Country Club of Little Rock Debutante Presentation. Held during the Christmas season.

The
Mobile Debutantes of 1986
request the pleasure of your company
at the
thirty-fourth Annual Camellia Ball
on
Thursday, the twenty-seventh of November
at nine o'clock in the evening
Riverview Plaza
Mobile, Alabama

"Admit one" to southern society

110

Louisville
The Debutante Ball. Held just before Christmas; since 1931.

Memphis
The Holiday Ball. Held the weekend before Christmas.

Mobile
The Camellia Ball. Held the Saturday after Thanksgiving; since 1953.

Nashville
The Bal d'Hiver. Held in February by Kappa Alpha Theta. Nashville's oldest deb presentation.
The Eve of Janus Ball. Held New Year's Eve; sponsored by Delta Delta Delta.

New Orleans
Le Debut. Held in August.
The Debutante Club Presentation. Held around Thanksgiving.
The Courts of Mardi Gras. Young ladies are honored by the members of various Mardi Gras krewes. Oldest-line daughters usually come out at one of the deb presentations plus "lead" one or two krewe balls.

Vintage Mardi Gras costume design, New Orleans

State of North Carolina
Terpsichorean Ball. Held in Raleigh over the Labor Day weekend. One hundred and twenty-five debs from all over the state represent its most prominent families.

Richmond
Richmond German. Held Christmas week at the Commonwealth Club; since 1832.

SOCIAL MONARCHY IN DIXIE

One of the most superlative social statements made in the Southland occurs each winter in the port cities of Mobile and New Orleans, the courts of Mardi Gras. At the heart of Mardi Gras is Deep South social history in the making and remaking year after year after year.

If you belong to the Order of Old Southern Families in these locales, you're well aware that Mardi Gras means much more than mirth, frivolity, and revelry. It represents the annual promenade of the social upper crust under the auspices of socially elite "mystic societies." But even more socially significant to you and your peers, Mardi Gras heralds the final act of the annual drama of social clout, made public, no less: the an-

King and Queen of 1987 Mardi Gras, Mobile, Alabama

Mardi Gras "throws"

nouncement of Mardi Gras royalty, better known as "the Court." In Mobile there's one reigning court for the citywide celebration; in New Orleans there's a court for each krewe. Yes, Virginia, you *can* be a monarch in America.

In these cities, being selected Mardi Gras royalty is *the* social coup for any debutante or bachelor. With the revelation of the court(s), not only does it become clear to the entire city whether your family measures up against society's yardstick, but everybody also learns exactly how your family measures up against the others in the running.

Despite these weighty social implications, the results are far from surprising, since the same families have been jousting in this courtly rivalry for generations. Don't forget: This is a social tradition, not a popularity contest or a beauty pageant. It doesn't matter how gregarious or fetching you are. If you don't have the lineage and a long family history of supporting the carnival organizations (and extremely deep pockets), you have nary a chance of becoming Mardi Gras royalty, at least not in the big-league mystic societies, which are the only ones that *really* count.

If you have what it takes, the biggest suspense is not whether you'll be invited to become royalty, but for which year and for which distinction (in New Orleans, for which krewes; in Mobile, for which title—king, queen, knight, lady in waiting, *et al*). After all, this social ritual runs in the families of the Order, which means if you made Court, you're no doubt following in the footsteps of your mama and daddy and their mamas and daddies, and so forth.

PROPRIETY IN DIXIE SOCIETY

Helping others has long been a lifetime avocation for raised-right Southerners. Not only do we consider "showing charity" the godly thing to do (and you know how deep those principles run), it's only natural that we show charitable concern for fellow Southerners. Also, this propensity for giving a hand probably has more than a little to do with the fact that the Southland is pretty much one big extended family. No wonder showing brotherly love comes naturally to folks in Dixie.

In fact, being deficient in the lend-a-helping-hand department is a grievous sin, not only of moral proportions, but of social ones, as well. The unwritten code is: the higher your social station in the Southland, the more you need to work for a good cause. If you're not willing to roll up your sleeves and work like a field hand in the name of a good cause, don't be surprised if your good standing in the ranks of Good Folk slips a few notches. You were blessed enough to have more than enough; how about returning in kind?

Some of the most ardent practitioners of this ethic are the ladies of southern society. Without the endless corps of volunteers that these gentlewomen of the South have assembled and led, life would be very different in Dixie. Name a noble cause—community service, education, the arts, preservation, health, and religion—and you can be sure that leagues of southern ladies have wielded considerable effort and yielded considerable results with the fervor of a zealot, the organization of a corporation, and the discipline of the military. You can be sure that their best-laid plans have grandly succeeded, under budget and over goal.

You can be sure they did it with plenty of southern grace and charm and without being undignified, pushy, or otherwise ruffling feathers (except maybe a few of their own). You can count on it because, like most well-bred southern ladies, they're honors graduates of the iron-fist-in-velvet-glove school, a tradition unique to Dixie and as ingrained in our culture as the southern accent. Where else could a lady move mountains and never work up a sweat, much less perspire? Well, it happens regularly all over the Southland.

114

USING ACADEMIA TO MAKE THE SOCIAL GRADE

What kind of social statement does your college make for you in Dixie? Say no more than the name of your alma mater, and Southlanders can get an easy fix on your social *savoir-faire*. This is why mamas and daddies who are, shall we say, socially *aware* do not take lightly their child's selection of a college (and vice versa).

Not that academics aren't a consideration for college-material Southerners. But since we're such *sociable* a folk, you can bet your last goober that a school's social profile is going to figure prominently in the picture.

See what sorts of social statements are being made with the following college selection scenarios:

"It will be good for James/Jennifer to expand his/her horizons outside the South."

Translation: My child is going to a Northeastern name school because it's socially prestigious.

Likely choices: Ivy League school, Seven Sisters school. (Note: Many Southlanders still take a rather dim view of shipping kids up north to get educated, even if it *is* the age of the New South.)

"My child is going to a quality southern school with kids from quality southern families like ours."

Translation: My child is going to an exclusive country club school in the South with all her/his prep school pals.

Likely choices: private institutions such as Centre, Davidson, Duke, Hampden-Sydney (all male), Millsaps, University of the South, Vanderbilt, Wake Forest, Washington and Lee. Although a public school, William and Mary otherwise fits into this category.

"My daughter needs a quality education in a refined, close-knit environment."

Translation: Liz is going to an old southern girls' school.

Likely choices: Mary Baldwin, Converse, Hollins, Meredith, Mississippi University for Women, Sophie Newcomb, Queens, Randolph-Macon, St. Mary's, Salem, Agnes Scott, Sweet Briar, Wesleyan.

"My child can get a well-rounded education right here in the South." (Also known as, *"What's wrong with a B.A. from the University of Tennessee?"*)

Translation: I'll buy my child a four-year degree and maybe a sorority/fraternity membership, but I won't float the national debt to do it.

Likely choices: State universities or colleges.

"Will needs to grow up a little."

Translation: Will's going to a military school where they'll beat his rump if he misbehaves.

Likely choices: The Citadel, Virginia Military Institute.

"My Bobbette excels in social pursuits; academics are not her forte."

Translation: My child is a good kid, but she couldn't make over 900 on the SAT unless she was visited with a miracle.

Likely choices: Open-admissions state universities or regional colleges glad to get the tuition.

A final note: Don't think that attending a public university is going to sabotage your social approval quotient in Dixie, no matter how socially prominent your family. On the contrary, it's a popular choice for plenty of youth from the South's old-line peerage. But you do need to adhere to a few critical guidelines if you're serious about passing social muster:

1. Be sure to attend the most prestigious university in the state. It will also probably be the oldest and will probably have a respectable liberal arts program. It will probably *not* be the state ag-tech school.

2. Be sure you pledge a sorority or fraternity, and only one that's well thought of. Till your dying day, you'll be graded on your response to, "You went to Chapel Hill? What sorority (fraternity) were you in?" And to those who care enough to inquire, the only response worse than the name of a crummy sorority or fraternity is, "I wasn't in one."

CHAPTER SIX

What's Cooking Down South

A Nonstop Feast of Southern Cuisine and Tips for Sharing in Our Bounty

Seems as of late folks in the rest of the world finally have latched onto what we've known about Down South for centuries: the eating's great, and biscuits and red-eye gravy are just the start of our vast repertoire of culinary classics. Any doubting Thomases need only to conduct a Southland taste test or brush up on their trend watching (Don't even *try* to count all the southern cookbooks Yankee publishers have issued recently).

Around here, we're blessed with what noted southern food expert Camille Glenn calls "an embarrassment of riches." Our motherland is the mother lode. And with a plentitude of cultures in our heritage, our gastronomic passions have become permanent landmarks on the southern landscape. For a guided tour through Dixie food lore, turn the page.

CLASSIC SOUTHERN-STYLE CUISINE

There's far more to our proud, prolific legacy of food than our famous southern home cooking, but it's those traditional southern-style meals that have come to be synonymous with the Southland.

This classic style of cooking is a gastronomic lesson in our Dixie foods. Old World food fare, New World bounty (like corn, turkeys, possum), and foods from Africa (such as watermelons, okra, and benne or sesame seed), the West Indies, and the Southern Hemisphere were stirred into our culinary stock pot by resourceful southern cooks. They shaped a cuisine that became—and remains—a legend among those who know what good food is.

Whether grand-scale or routine, the classic Southern Style of cooking is an unforgettable feast of the freshest, finest, and most honest ingredients faithfully prepared according to treasured methods. While there's no doubt that fast food, frozen entrees, and calorie counting have made their marks upon the supper table in today's Dixie, most Southerners still try our darnedest to make time and room for meals the way God meant them to be: made our way, from scratch.

You really haven't lived until you've had a genuine home-cooked, southern-style meal. But if you don't yet belong to the land of the living, there's still hope.

BASIC TRUTHS ABOUT HOME COOKING SOUTHERN STYLE

■ **Tastes great because the ingredients come straight from the garden or barnyard.**

Using techno-grown and processed provisions just won't get you to the same gastronomic nirvana. After all, real southern cooking is real country cooking, originally made by and for Southlanders whose foodstuffs were as close as the backyard and barnyard (and the pantry and the smokehouse). Even though few of us have chickens or pigs behind the house any longer, finding fresh foodstuffs is not a hopeless cause as long as you grow your own vegetables (or know where to find them) and know where to look for wild game (in the woods or your deer-hunting neighbor's freezer).

■ **Takes a long time to prepare and cook.**

You don't just "whip up" a genuine southern-style meal. The original versions were days in the making and if you're aiming to replicate one of them, then clear your calendar. That country ham took about a year to cure, overnight to soak, and a few more hours to glaze (or slice and fry). That barbecue has to roast in an open pit at least twelve hours, with lots of basting. Those vegetables have to be picked, cleaned, prepared, and slow-cooked. Those sweets and desserts don't come in a box; neither do those cat-head biscuits. And don't forget the condiments you "put up" over a couple of weeks last summer to round out your meal.

■ **Sticks to your bones.**

Nobody has ever claimed that southern-style cooking would make good spa food. Remember, it was originally made to keep folks' engines running steady over a hard day's work out of doors. For a meal high in protein and carbohydrates, help yourself to some southern cooking. So for a meal that's low-fat, low salt, or low sugar, you'd better look elsewhere, like maybe California.

Not every meal we eat Down South these days is a genuine whole-hog version of yesteryear; seems the New South lifestyle often precludes a steady diet of our classic downhome cooking. But often enough, we find ourselves celebrating our culinary heritage with a proper Old South meal at home, especially a Sunday dinner (that means lunch) and sometimes a country breakfast.

The whole family attends. So do relatives and lucky friends. Everybody leaves fat and happy, and glad to be a Southerner.

"COMPANY'S COMING" SUNDAY DINNER
A mighty respectable rendition of the old-time Sunday spread.
*Recipes to follow

Southern fried chicken*

Wildflower honey

Iced tea

Buttermilk
(for Granny)

Sweet potato pie*

Sorghum
(made by Jaycees)

Pecan pie
(pecans came from
Aunt Hallie's orchards)

Buttermilk biscuits*

Toothpicks

Cornbread

Iced tea spoons

Butter

Green beans, butterbeans,
turnip greens, and field peas
(all homegrown and slow-cooked
with salt meat)

Fried okra
(pod of the Gods)

Vintage tablecloth
and cloth napkins
(from Grandmother's
trousseau)

Fresh sliced tomatoes on old
pressed glass saucer
("free with box top of Crystal
Oats")

Peanut butter
and jelly sandwich
(for William Jr.)

"Damask Rose"
sterling silver flatware
by Oneida (Mama's)

Pepper
sauce
(made by
pastor's
wife)

Pan gravy
(made from
fried chicken
drippings)

White rice

■ Southern Fried Chicken

Whether you buy whole chickens and cut them up yourself or choose special cuts (breasts, thighs), select the leanest, smallest bird(s) you can find. (There are no more "barnyard" chickens to be fried the same day they are killed, but just remember that young and lean is better than old and fat, and do the best you can.) Soak the pieces in lightly salted cold water for an hour or more to extract the blood. Drain and pat dry, then rub with salt and pepper. In a deep, heavy black skillet, melt enough shortening to reach a depth of ½ inch or so and add 3 or 4 tablespoons of bacon grease to it. Put a cup or more of flour and ½ teaspoon each of salt and pepper in a paper sack and shake each piece of chicken individually in the sack until it is well coated. Then lay the pieces gently into the medium-hot grease (sizzling but not smoking). Don't crowd the pieces. When golden brown and crispy-looking on one side, turn with tongs and cook to the same state on the other side. Depending on the size of the chicken and the heat of the grease, the total cooking time should be 20 to 30 minutes. An uncovered skillet will make drier, crispier chicken. When done, lay the pieces out on absorbent paper to soak up excess grease.

—*Southern Food,* by John Egerton, © 1987 by John Egerton. Reprinted by permission of Alfred A. Knopf, Inc.

WISH UPON A BONE

Every bona fide fried chicken dinner in Dixie concludes with the wishbone ritual: two diners face off, each holding one "leg" of the bare wishbone (held thumbs up). Each makes a wish. Both then pull the bone until it snaps in two. Legend holds that whoever ends up with the longer piece will have his wish come true. A favorite ritual for kids Down South.

■ Southern Buttermilk Biscuits

2 cups all-purpose flour, plus more as needed
¼ teaspoon baking soda
1 tablespoon baking powder
1 teaspoon salt
6 tablespoons lard or solid vegetable shortening
¾ cup buttermilk

1. Sift the dry ingredients into a roomy bowl. Cut in the shortening with a pastry blender or a fork until the mixture has the texture of coarse meal. Add the buttermilk and mix with your hand, lightly but thoroughly. Add a little more flour if the dough is too sticky. Knead for 1 minute. Wrap in wax paper or foil and refrigerate until well chilled, at least 20 minutes.
2. Preheat the oven to 450°F.
3. Roll the dough out ½ inch thick on a lightly floured surface or pastry cloth. (Always roll from the center out for tender, crisp biscuits.) Cut the dough into the desired size biscuits.
4. Place the biscuits on a dark baking sheet and bake until golden brown, 10 to 12 minutes.

Makes 25 to 30 biscuits.

—*The Heritage of Southern Cooking* by Camille Glenn

■ Sweet Potato Pie

3 large sweet potatoes
2 tablespoons butter
½ cup sugar
½ teaspoon cinnamon
½ teaspoon nutmeg
1 egg
2 egg whites
4 teaspoons sugar

Boil potatoes until soft. Peel and mash well with 2 tablespoons butter. Add sugar, cinnamon, nutmeg, and egg, well beaten. Fill cooked pastry shell and cover with meringue made of beaten egg whites and 4 teaspoons of sugar. Brown in medium oven. Serves 6.

—*Charleston Receipts*

COUNTRY BREAKFAST SOUTHERN STYLE

Tradition holds that you don't skimp on breakfast Down South. Lots of Southlanders to this day eat a substantial breakfast, including a hearty serving of meat (even fried chicken). Here's an old favorite, good for breakfast or a lazy weekend brunch.

MENU

Sliced country ham*
Smoked sausage
Red-eye gravy
Grits
Old Virginia Spoonbread**
Fried and scrambled eggs
Sliced tomatoes
Biscuits
Buckwheat pancakes
Fried apples
Fig jam** and cane syrup
Coffee

*Not just any old ham will do. You want real, honest-to-goodness cured country ham, which you should slice and fry.
**Recipe follows

■ Old Virginia Spoonbread

4 cups milk
1 cup yellow cornmeal
1½ tablespoons salt
½ cup water

4 egg yolks, beaten
4 egg whites
⅛ teaspoon cream of tartar

Scald milk. Mix salt and cornmeal with water and stir into milk. Cook until thickened. Remove from heat. Add a small amount of hot cornmeal to egg yolks, then stir yolks into hot cornmeal.

Add cream of tartar to egg whites. Whip until stiff but moist. Fold whites into cornmeal and pour into a 2-quart greased casserole pan. Bake at 350° until light brown and a knife inserted in center comes out clean. Serves 6.

—from *Virginia Seasons*

■ Fig Jam

6 quarts boiling water
6 quarts fresh figs
Sugar

1 quart water
8 slices lemon

Pour boiling water over figs; let stand 15 minutes. Drain and thoroughly rinse in cold water. Pat dry; remove stems. Crush and measure figs; place in a large Dutch oven. Add ½ cup sugar for each cup of crushed figs. Add 1 quart water. Bring to a rapid boil; reduce heat, and simmer, uncovered, 3 hours or until thickened, stirring occasionally.

Ladle jam into hot sterilized jars, leaving ¼-inch headspace; add a slice of lemon to each jar. Cover at once with metal lids, and screw on bands. Process in a boiling-water bath 10 minutes. Yield: 8½ pints.

—from *Southern Living* magazine

RITUALS WITH VICTUALS:
TABLE ETIQUETTE DOWN SOUTH

OPENING COMMENT

Always say the blessing before you begin the meal. ("Good grub, good meat, good God, let's eat" does not qualify.)

■ Table-Top How-to

Serving savoir-faire (two-methods):

1. Pass to the right. When you're passed a serving dish, hold it so your neighbor on the left can help him or herself. Then pass to your neighbor on the right so he/she can do the same for you. Also known as "boardinghouse style,"* this is the most formal and orderly method and is always used when several people come to dinner or supper.

2. Serve others from the bowl or platter closest to you as they hand you their plates from across the table. This is a more informal (and haphazard) method, but works fine if there aren't too many people at the table.

Do's and don'ts for doctoring up your food:

1. *Do* put butter, salt, and pepper or red-eye gravy on your grits. *Do not* sprinkle sugar or pour syrup on them.

2. *Do* sprinkle pepper sauce on your greens.

3. *Do* ladle pot likker on your corn bread, meat, or vegetables.

4. *Do* pour cane syrup or sorghum on vegetables or breads, if your heart so desires.

When to use your fingers at mealtime:

1. When eating fried chicken (be sure to frequently lick your fingers).

2. When eating bacon.

3. When using your bread as "push bread" (to coax your food onto your fork) or to "sop up" tasty liquids (gravy, pot likker, and so forth) from your plate.

4. When crumbling corn bread into your glass of buttermilk.

Utensil utilization:

1. Hold your fork in your right hand. Rest your knife across the top rim of the plate. Do not use the European style of fork-in-left, knife-in-right unless you wish to put on airs of well-traveled sophistication.

2. To cut your meat, switch the fork from your right hand to your left and put the knife in your now-empty right hand. Hold the fork, tines down, and pierce the meat. Cut with the knife and replace it across the plate rim. Switch the fork back to your right hand, tines up. Eat and enjoy.

3. Use a napkin, not your sleeve or the back of your hand, to wipe your mouth.

■ **And Remember**

- A southern lady should always eat with dainty bites and leave some of her food uneaten. It is *most* unladylike to exhibit a voracious appetite in public, even if this is indeed the case.

- Except in the most sophisticated of restaurants, gentlemen may use a toothpick in Dixie after leaving the table. They should not, however, conduct an overly enthusiastic search-and-destroy mission. A southern lady still refrains from such boorish behavior—at least in public.

- It is incontrovertibly bad manners to emit a burp or belch while at the table.

- Don't get up from the table until your hostess/host has acknowledged the meal is over.

- Thank your hostess/host for a real good meal.

---

*Not to be confused with a "boardinghouse reach," an over-the-table retrieval of a dish.

WHAT EVERY GOOD SOUTHERN COOK KEEPS HANDY

If you're going to cook southern-style meals, your efforts will be sorely lacking if you don't have our standard pantry staples on hand. Every southern cook worth her or his salt pork uses them and uses them often. Here's what to put on your shopping list:

■ Store Bought

White grits
Cornmeal: white and yellow
Winter-wheat flour (the secret to our light biscuits and cakes)
Syrups: cane, sorghum
Lard
Fatback/salt pork
Tabasco Sauce
Cast iron cookware (for deep-fat frying and for baking corn bread)
Biscuit cutter
Paper sacks (for flour-coating chicken to be fried)
Bourbon whiskey

■ Put Up

Preserves and jams: peach, fig, pear
Jellies: dewberry, blackberry, scuppernong, quince, pepper
Butters: apple or peach
Spiced peaches
Relishes: hot pepper, tomato, Vidalia onion, chow-chow
Pickles: watermelon rind, bread and butter, squash, okra
Beans: green (pole/snap/string), butter (lima)
Field peas (crowder/cow/black-eyed/lady)
Pepper sauce
Sourwood honey
Pecans
Muscadine or scuppernong wine

FIVE FAVORITE SOUTHERN PIES

Pecan
Chess
Sweet Potato
Black Bottom
Peach

127

TAKING IT TO THE LIMIT: MORE THAN MERELY DOWNHOME

For many of us, the mere sight of them is enough to last a lifetime, but others of us were raised to appreciate what we'll classify as the backwoods delicacies of the Southland: poke sallet, chitterlings, possum, and the like. Time was, southern folks who had to make do did just that with this sort of food fare. Nowadays, it's more a matter of taste (and pride) than pure necessity, as anyone who's ever attended the Cosby Ramp Festival in Cosby, Tennessee, or the Chitlin Strut in Salley, South Carolina, for example, can confirm.

If you have an adventuresome appetite and care to sample such of our original foods, don't look for them in the high-rent districts. City folk don't eat them (or own up to it). Instead, find yourself a country cousin or a food festival* to dish you up what you've been missing all these years. It'll be a treat you won't be likely to forget.

Poke sallet: a bitter green that grows wild around the South and is slow-cooked like turnip greens.

Ramp: Appalachian delicacy (also known as wild leek) with the pungency of an onion, garlic, or leek. Served raw, fried, boiled, or scrambled with eggs.

Chitterlings (chitlins): pig intestines that are turned inside out, braided, boiled, and then fried. Not for the faint-hearted.

Cracklings: crispy leftovers from the rendering of pork fat during hog slaughtering. Cracklings make a tasty addition to corn bread.

Pigs feet, hog jowls: the former are often pickled in brine for later consumption.

Cooter: turtle. Boil the cooter in the shell and use the meat for soups, stews, or casseroles.

Possum: opossum. Best when baked.

Frog legs: served batter-fried.

*See listings later in this chapter.

BEYOND GRITS AND GREENS: FIVE-STAR SOUTHERN CUISINES

Now that you know that the classic style of southern cooking is the end-all and be-all for the hearts, minds, and stomachs of the Southland, you need to know something else. There's more to southern food than our famous homestyle meals, God bless them. We've got plenty more culinary trump cards up our sleeves: regional cuisines like Cajun and Creole, coastal fare (à la Carolina Low Country and Gulf Coast), specialties such as barbecue, catfish, Brunswick stew, and Kentucky burgoo, plus scores of original Southland delights. All are worth a trip from anywhere, so make your travel plans now.

Oysters Bienville
Red Beans and Rice
Jambalaya
Crawfish Bisque
Oysters Rockefeller
Blackened Redfish
Shrimp Creole
Trout Amandine
Chicory Coffee
Po Boy Sandwiches
Shrimp Remoulade
Pompano en Papillote
Beignets
Bread Pudding

■ Creole and Cajun.

Credit Louisiana's cornucopia of cultures (French, Spanish, Anglo-Saxon, African, Caribbean, and more) and its fertile land and waterways for these two legendary edible legacies. Think of New Orleans's famed Creole cuisine as the more cosmopolitan of the pair and of Cajun cooking as its spicier, bayou-country cousin (the latter glorified by Cajun chef Paul Prudhomme). Both maintain a distinct allegiance to traditional French cookery, but their ingredients (most importantly, seafood), seasonings, and style are pure native Louisiana. We can thank Louisiana for such contributions as:

Gumbo
Crawfish Étouffée

■ Cuisines of the Atlantic and Gulf Coasts

Less faddish than Louisiana cookery but worthy of equal admiration are the traditional cuisines of the coastal South. With the cultures of French and Spanish settlers in evidence, the fruits of the sea (oysters, crab, shrimp, and saltwater fish) in fresh and plentiful supply, and the essence of Old South flavoring it all, it's small wonder that generations of coastal Southerners have savored and handed down such favorites as these:

She-Crab Soup (South Carolina and Georgia)
Baked Red Snapper (Gulf and South Atlantic coasts)
Fried Crab Claws (Alabama)
Baked Shad (Carolinas and Georgia)

NOT-SO-SECRET KEY INGREDIENTS TO LOUISIANA COOKING

Filé powder: Made from ground sassafras leaves. A thickening and flavoring agent often used in making gumbo.

Okra: If you don't swear by filé powder, then the pod of the gods is the power and glory of your gumbos.

Crab boil: Spice mixes that are added to the water in which crabs, crawfish, and shrimp are boiled. Louisianans have been loyal to Zatarain's brand of ready-made crab boil for nearly a century.

Cayenne pepper: The ultimate way to spice up your Cajun cooking, particularly soups and stews. If you're brave, omit the olive and make a K-Paul-style Cajun martini with a cayenne pepper instead.

Tabasco Sauce: The gold standard of hot sauces. Adds fiery zest to all sorts of foods.

Crawfish: Small freshwater crustaceans that are distant relatives of the lobster. Their tail meat is a key ingredient in many Louisiana recipes and is also a favorite when served fresh-boiled, like shrimp.

Cane syrup: Extracted and boiled sugar cane juice; often added to Louisiana recipes.

Andouille: Cajun-made smoked sausage used as seasoning meat for recipes like jambalaya. The original article was made from hog entrails.

Tasso: Another Cajun-made seasoning meat. Made from pork; also known as Cajun ham.

Deviled Crab (Gulf and Atlantic coasts)

West Indies Salad (Alabama)

Crab Norfolk (Virginia)

Shrimp Pie (South Carolina)

Red Drum Stew and Pine Bark Stew (Atlantic coast)

Smoked Mullet (North Carolina and Virginia)

■ Wild Game

Hunting used to be the primary means of putting meat on the table in Dixie. Nowadays, it's mainly an opportunity for good old boys to stomp around in the woods or flyways with their buddies and whoop it up. Not that they don't take hunting seriously, however. It may be more sport than necessity for this generation, but you won't find a rank amateur in any group of southern hunters.

Quite naturally, our southern prowess on the hunt is matched by our southern savvy in the kitchen. If it moves, not only do we know how to kill it, we know how to make a meal out of it that's some kind of good. Skim a few southern cookbooks, and you'll see more than sufficient evidence:

Roast Wild Duck: stuffed with apple and potato dressing, basted with sherry, and served with wild rice.

Squirrel: fried, in casserole, or in stew (once a standard ingredient in Brunswick stews and Kentucky burgoos).

Venison Steak: broiled and served with a hot wine sauce and grits and gravy.

Raccoon: roasted with sweet potatoes, chopped vegetables, and seasonings and served in its own pan gravy.

Dove and Oyster Pie: doves stuffed and layered with oysters and baked with seasonings in pastry.

Quail: sautéed in butter and baked with a sherry or wine baste.

FIVE-STAR SPECIALTIES OF THE SOUTH

To indulge in all the creative cookery the South has to offer, you'll have to do a little traveling. Many of our finest treats aren't found everywhere in Dixie. More than a few of them are local or regional phenomena whose renown far eclipses their availability. But without exception, they're worth going out of your way for and they're definitely worth the wait.

■ Barbecue.

Of all the delights of the southern diet, barbecue is the most passionately debated method of preparing meat. Since it goes without saying that a southern meal isn't genuine or respectable unless there's meat on the plate, and since barbecuing dates back to the early days of our settlements, a discussion about barbecue should never be considered mere speculation.

Bona fide southern barbecue demands three things: pork shoulder or ribs (beef in Texas), an outdoor cooking pit, and a sauce with which to baste the meat. While this sounds simple, what makes barbecue such a mysterious and controversial topic is the multiplicity of methods employed to make and serve it. Therein also lies its pleasures.

■ Country Stews: Brunswick Stew and Kentucky Burgoo

The bounty of the South is readily apparent in these two similar renderings of a native meat-and-vegetable stew. Often served as an accompaniment to barbecue, they're equally bound to provoke debate. Predictably, no one agrees about where the first was concocted (Georgia, North Carolina, or Virginia), about the proper way to make them (the squirrel-versus-chicken debate is a twentieth-century twist to an already variable list of ingredients), and which recipe is the best.

One thing is for certain, however; no one ever went hungry after downing a round of either. With half the garden, barnyard, and wildwoods represented in their contents and a consistency so thick you can eat them with a fork, our country stews are edible proof that we Southerners don't take good food lightly.

■ Catfish

Put all of those notions of nasty scavenger fish out of your mind and pop a morsel of pond-raised catfish in your mouth instead. The lowly catfish ain't what she used to be. Today she's

VARIATIONS ON THE BARBECUE THEME

This is a simple introduction to what has become a complicated subject. There's food for debate in it all.

■ What to cook

Traditionalists prefer pork shoulder or a slab of pork ribs. Others opt for beef brisket or even lamb (which traditionalists consider pure hogwash).

■ How to cook it

About the only thing barbecuists agree upon is that slow cooking is essential, up to twelve hours for pork shoulder. Up for controversy: the coals (hickory wood versus charcoal), the basting sauce (vinegar sauce versus tomato and vinegar sauce versus mustard sauce or other secret ingredients) and when to/not to baste.

■ How to serve it

First, there's the issue of the meat. Some serve it sliced, others serve it chopped, and yet others serve it pulled in pieces from the shoulder (you may have a choice in the matter at some barbecues). Furthermore, there's a question of whether outside meat (dark meat) or inside meat (white meat) is best. Next, there's the debate whether to serve it on buns or bread (two slices of white) or alongside the latter.

Then, there's the matter of whether to add a final ladle of sauce, to provide it on the side, or not at all.

Lest all this sounds confusing, know that the final result is definitely worth the effort. It takes only one finger-licking feast of expertly made barbecue to convince you, at which time you'll think you've died and gone to heaven.

Lucky Southerners who live in the "southern barbecue belt" (which winds through parts of Alabama, Arkansas, Georgia, South Carolina, North Carolina, Kentucky, and Tennessee) get to taste the glories of barbecue whenever the spirit moves them. Around these neighborhoods, the brethren frequently can be found making a quick pilgrimage to their barbecue stand of choice or congregating in the name of civic or religious causes with a barbecue fund-raiser or festival. Two of the most gargantuan barbecue festivals occur annually in the rival barbecue capitals of Memphis, Tennessee, and Owensboro, Kentucky.

If you live too far from the holy land of barbecue for regular worship, fear not. You now can have southern-style barbecue air-expressed to your home and can even buy it in your grocer's frozen food case (see the "Dixie Hall of Fame" later in this chapter). Either should suffice until your next journey to your favorite stop on the barbecue belt.

the darling of diners everywhere—not just the South—to the tune of hundreds of millions of pounds a year.

Give thanks to southern ingenuity for using aquaculture to put one of our favorite foods within easy reach. Primarily grown in the Mississippi Delta region (Belzoni, Mississippi, is the "Catfish Capital of the World") and fed a pampered diet of corn, soybeans, and nutrients, you need only taste a southern-bred catfish to see what the fuss is all about.

The most fitting way to go about this is to pay a visit to a Down-South catfish house in the country (often located beside a lake or river). Don't expect frills; folks in these establish-

ments prefer to stick to the basics, which they do commendably. This includes cornmeal-battered, deep-fried catfish and plump hush puppies, with accompaniments of coleslaw, fresh onion slices, pitchers of iced tea, and friendly southern-style service.

THE VIDALIA ONION: TRÈS CHIC TREAT

Move over, Georgia peach. There's another lip-smacking celebrity in town, the sweet Vidalia onion. It's in such demand that peach sales are the pits, by comparison. A sweet peach is rarely in limited supply; a genuine sweet Vidalia onion always is.

Like Smithfield hams, these eponymous onions come from one place and one place only: Vidalia, Georgia. The soil around Vidalia is almost devoid of sulfur (the culprit behind a typical onion's searing bite). Ergo, a Vidalia onion is a mild and sweet delight to eat, even right out of your hand.

Nowhere else on the face of the earth is such an onion found. So for a few months each summer, when the Vidalia is in season, plain folk and connoisseurs alike clamor for a supply of Vidalias and then retreat to their kitchens to devise yet another recipe for the pearly delight. We heartily recommend you do the same. If your grocer doesn't stock them, have a grower ship them (see "Earthy Delights," page 154).

HOW-TO BOOKS FOR COOKING UP YOUR OWN SOUTHERN SPECIALTIES

Ready to try your hand with some southern cooking of your own? Well, we're more than happy to share our recipes with you and, quite naturally, a little commentary as well. You can't go wrong with these cookbook standouts:

The Heritage of Southern Cooking, by Camille Glenn, published by Workman Publishing Company.

Southern Food, by John Egerton, published by Alfred A. Knopf.

Bill Neal's Southern Cooking, by Bill Neal, published by the University of North Carolina Press.

Craig Claiborne's Southern Cooking, by Craig Claiborne, published by Outlet Book Company.

Grace Hartley's Southern Cookbook, by Grace Hartley, published by Galahad Books.

Miss Mary's Down-home Cooking, by Diana Dalass, published by New American Library.

White Trash Cooking, by Ernest Mickler, published by the Jargon Society and Ten Speed Press.

Chef Paul Prudhomme's Louisiana Kitchen, by Paul Prudhomme, published by William Morrow and Company, Inc.

The New Orleans Cookbook, by Rima and Richard Collin, published by Alfred A. Knopf.

Gracious Entertaining, Southern Style, by Daisy King, published by Rutledge Hill Press.

SOUTHERN STYLE #5: COUNTRY FOLK
They're walking away winners at the county fair.

Motherly hairdo (goes to Jeanette's Cut 'N Curl every Friday).

Her prize-winning pickles, in Ball canning jar, with a personalized label: "From the Kitchen of Doreen Walker."

Gimme cap.

J. C. Penney chambray snapfront workshirt.

Gruen watch with bracelet band.

Certificate for Best of Show for his Brahman bull (fifth year he's won).

Rattlesnake belt (killed it last year while hunting turkey).

Vinyl Ambassador bag (bought by mail-order).

Timex watch with Speidel Twistoflex band.

Dress made from Simplicity pattern #9876, poly/cotton no-iron blend.

In pockets: Swiss army pocket knife, RED MAN chew (a plug in his mouth, too), keys to Chevrolet pickup, house, and gates to various cow pastures, hand-tooled leather wallet (with his name on it), handkerchief.

Lee jeans.

From Baker's.

Redwing work boots.

The Southern Junior League Cook-book, published by David McKay Company.
Charleston Receipts, published by the Junior League of Charleston, South Carolina.
Recipe Jubilee! published by the Junior League of Mobile, Alabama.
River Road Recipes, published by the Junior League of Baton Rouge, Louisiana.
Kentucky Hospitality, published by the Kentucky Federation of Women's Clubs, Louisville, Kentucky.
Aunt Bee's Mayberry Cookbook, by Jim Clark and Ken Beck, with recipes edited by Julia M. Pitkin, published by Rutledge Hill Press.

DIXIE HALL OF FOOD FAME

Not only has southern foodlore established a name for itself, it boasts quite a few names that have become household words. These are the food and drink products that regularly grace many a Southerner's palate and pantry (and many a non–Southerner's, too). They're so much a part of life down here that we'd literally be losing the flavor of the Southland were they to disappear.

Fortunately, that's not likely, since nobody's expecting our appetite for these stars of southern foodlore to wane anytime soon. It's precisely because of their esteemed status that they belong to the prestigious Dixie Hall of Food Fame, our Who's Who of favorite and famous foods from the Southland.

■ **Dixie Hall of Food Famers and Their Hometowns**

Goo-Goo Clusters (Nashville)
Moon Pies [Deluxe Double Decker] (Chattanooga)
Elmer's Gold Brick candy bars (New Orleans)
King Leo Peppermint Sticks (Nashville)
Claxton Fruitcakes (Claxton, Georgia)
Golden Flake Cheese Curls ["Good as Gold"] (Birmingham)
Lance Nabs (Charlotte, North Carolina)
Slim Jim Beef Jerkys (Raleigh, North Carolina)
Tom's Peanuts (Columbus, Georgia)
Planters' Peanuts (Suffolk, Virginia)
Kentucky Fried Chicken (Corbin, Kentucky)
Popeye's Fried Chicken (New Orleans)
Coca-Cola [Classic] (Atlanta)
Royal Crown [RC] Cola (Columbus, Georgia)
Barq's Root Beer (Biloxi, Mississippi)
Jax Beer (New Orleans)
Dixie Beer (New Orleans)
Community Coffee (Baton Rouge, Louisiana)
Luzianne Coffee (New Orleans)
Maxwell House Coffee (Nashville)
White Lily Flour and Cornmeal Mix (Knoxville, Tennessee)

Martha White's Jim Dandy Grits ["Real Old-South flavor"] (Nashville)

Duncan Hines Cake Mixes (Bowling Green, Kentucky)

Dixie Crystals Sugar (Savannah)

Blue Plate Mayonnaise (New Orleans)

Bama Preserves and Jellies (Birmingham)

White House Apple Juice (Winchester, Virginia)

The Allens' Popeye Spinach (Siloam Springs, Arkansas)

Tabasco Sauce (Avery Island, Louisiana)

Bryan's Pork Sausage (West Point, Mississippi)

Zatarain's Crab Boil (New Orleans)

. . . And the Up to Your Ears in Peas Award unanimously goes to Allen Canning Company of Siloam Springs, Arkansas, which sells its black-eyed peas under *five* different labels: The Allens, Allens Homefolks, Kitch-n-Kraft, Allens Sunshine, and Allens East Texas Fair. Should these five not fully satisfy your pea-pickin' quota, they offer yet three more varieties of peas from which to choose.

DIXIE HALL OF FAME TRIVIA TEST

How much do you know about Dixie food that's done us proud? Take this test and see:

1. Name the ingredients in a Goo-Goo Cluster *Supreme*.
2. Name the Dixie-made product that's been an announced sponsor of Grand Ole Opry broadcasts for over forty years.
3. What major soft drink, originally concocted in New Bern, North Carolina, was first named "Brad's Drink"?
4. Which U.S. president is said to have proclaimed the coffee of Nashville's Maxwell House hotel as "Good to the last drop"? (Answers on page 142.)

HOW TO BRING A TASTE OF THE SOUTH TO YOUR HOUSE

No matter where you live, the good taste of the Southland is within easy reach. Thanks to mail order, no one need ever again be deprived of some of life's brightest moments. Count your blessings.

■ Delectables

Seckinger-Lee Cocktail Biscuits: These bite-size delicacies can enliven even the dullest party, because folks can't help but wax enthusiastic over the fabulous taste of these gourmet hors d'oeuvres. Their cheese, bacon-cheese, and butter pecan biscuits are soooo good that the tony Neiman Marcus and Bergdorf Goodman stores offer the entire line by mail order. So does the southern-based Reids of Charlotte: 800/998-9855.

Byrd's Benne Wafers, Benne Candy, and more: Byrd's "crisp, sweet, wafer-thin cookies" are a confectionary legend whose appeal comes from benne (sesame) seeds. The entire line of goodies is especially popular for gift giving. (Byrd Cookie Company, Post Office Box 13086, Savannah, GA 31406; 912/355-1716.)

Mrs. Hane's Moravian Cookies: Cookie aficionados throughout the United States concur. Evva Hane's crisp and "Flavor-Full" sugar cookies deserve all the superlative praise they receive. Made from an old family recipe, each delicate cookie is rolled, cut, and packaged by hand. Other varieties offered, too. (431 Friedburg Church Road, Clemmons, NC 27012; 919/764-1402.)

Goo-Goo Clusters and King Leo Stick Candy: Southerners get hooked on these candies early in life, so much so that the Standard Candy Company regularly ships them to yearning natives at addresses far and wide. The Goo-Goo Cluster is "Tennessee's unofficial Official Candy Bar since 1912." (Mail Order Department, Post Office Box 101025, Nashville, TN 37210; 800/226-4340.)

Gethsemani Farms Fruitcakes: Gourmet columns regularly provide accolades to the bourbon-laced, fruit-packed holiday fruitcakes made by the Trappist Monks at the Abbey of Gethsemani. So do consumers. Gethsemani Farms' volume of business is so large they have their own zip code. Cheese and fudge also available. (Trappist, KY 40051; 502/549-3117.)

Pepper Patch Tennessee Tipsy Fruitcake: As the name implies, theirs is a spirited fruitcake, with a liberal lacing of Jack Daniel's Tennessee Whiskey. More high spirits (sherry and triple-sec) come in the Pepper Patch's Williamsburg Orange Wine Cake. Both "made from scratch." (1250 Old Hillsboro Road, Franklin, TN 37064; 615/790-1012.)

■ **Pantry Prizes**

Prissy's of Vidalia: With a name like Prissy's, there's no mistaking the true ring of southern heritage in this inspired line of Vidalia-based condiments and mixes. Don't overlook the jams, jellies, and fruit butters traditional to Down South pantries. (Post Office Box 1213, Vidalia GA 30474; 800/673-7372.)

Callaway Gardens: Their Speckled Heart Grits, which include bits of the corn kernel heart, are commendable examples of great grits. Try also a slab of their smokehouse-cured pepper-coated bacon. Other southern food products, including a line of hard-to-find muscadine condiments, are also available. (Callaway Gardens Country Store, Pine Mountain, GA 31822; 800/282-8181.)

Pepper Patch: A showcase of inspired southern condiments, the entire Pepper Patch line is handmade, all-natural, and very intriguing. With such products as Jezebel Sauce, Spring Onion Jelly, Apple Relish, and Sweet Potato Butter, biscuits and crackers will never be the same again. (See prior address.)

The Mayhaw Tree products: Not everybody gets to savor the makings of the tart red Mayhaw berry, because the wild Mayhaw trees grow only in the swamps and bogs of southwest Georgia. The harvest is gathered by hand and scooped out of the water with fishnets. The results well justify the arduous means: jelly, wine jelly, syrup, ham sauce, and salad dressing, all made with the precious Mayhaw. (Post Office Box 525, Colquitt, GA 31737; 800/677-3227.)

Tabasco Country Store: Capitalizing upon its ever-growing cult status, the folks behind the famous hot sauce now operate the Tabasco Country Store, which offers every sort of signature product imaginable (edible and non) along with interesting lore. (Avery Island, LA 70513; 800/634-9599 weekdays.)

Café du Monde: Anyone who's ever tasted the nectar of French Market Coffee with Chicory knows the meaning of bliss. Anyone who hasn't can come close, merely by making a phone call to Café du Monde. You'd be well-advised to also order their mix for beignets, those inimitable French doughnuts. (1039 Decatur Street, New Orleans, LA 70116; 504/581-2914.)

■ **Smoked Meats**

S. Wallace Edwards & Sons Virginia Hams: Three generations of Edwards have been tending the family business, with extraordinary results. Edwards hams have been winning awards and kudos for just about as long as they've been dry curing and hickory smoking hams. Smoked link sausage, bacon, and a variety of prepared foods are also available. (Highway 10, Box 25, Surry, VA 23883; 800/222-4267.)

The Smithfield Collection: From the town whose name is synonymous with ham comes an offering of succulent hams that are dry cured and smoked with oak, hickory, and apple woods. Hickory-smoked duck, pheasant, and turkey are featured also, as is an array of complements for the meal, including sidemeats. (Post Office Box 487, Smithfield, VA 23430; 800/628-2242.)

Mayo Sausage Company: Since 1932 the Mayo family has been pleasing Tennesseans with its dry-cured, hickory-smoked pork sausage and similarly prepared hams and bacon. Their products are so good that several companies depend upon the Mayos to make their own branded sausage for them. (Write: Balz Brothers Packing Company, 1612 Elm Hill Pike, Nashville, TN 37210; 800/251-1050.)

Maurice's Flying Pig Gourmet Barbecue: South Carolina's king of barbecue will ship his famous pit-cooked pork barbecue (chopped or ribs), sauce, and more anywhere in the United States, even Alaska and Hawaii. (Call 1/800-MAURICE.)

■ Earthy Delights

Vidalia Onions: These delicacies may be mail ordered from any number of shippers including *Vidalia Sweets,* whose onions "are organically grown," 800/537-7009; and Bland Farms; 800/VIDALIA.

Pecans: Pecan growers abound in the South, especially the Deep South. Three popular sources are: *Ellis Brothers Pecans* ("We're Nuts . . . To Sell This Low") Vienna, GA 31092; 800/635-0616; *Sherard Plantation Pecans,* Post Office Box 75, Sherard, MS 38669; 800/647-5518; and *Priester's Pecans,* Fort Deposit, AL 36032; 800/277-3226.

Peanuts: Who would dare dispute that goobers are a quintessentially southern food? Fans from anywhere can get their fill from *Virginia Diner Peanuts,* a frequent food writers' choice, Post Office Box 1030, Wakefield, VA 23888; 800/868-6887; or *A & B Milling Company, Inc.,* Box 327, Enfield, NC 27823; 800/843-0105.

■ Louisiana Fare

Sea Island Mercantile and Provisioning, Ltd.: Seafood, low-country style, can now be delivered to your door, as can freshly harvested coastal shrimp and oysters from clean, protected waters. The Carolina She-Crab Soup, Sweetmarsh Oyster Stew, and Littleneck Clam Chowder are favorites. Recipes, condiments, more. (Post Office Box 100, Beaufort, SC, 29901; 800/735-3215.)

K-Paul's: Everything you need to produce an authentic Louisiana meal (with the accent on Cajun) is available from the enterprising Paul Prudhomme. Meats, spices, prepared entrées, recipes, wares, videos, and folklore aplenty. (K-Paul's Louisiana Kitchen, Post Office Box 23342, New Orleans, LA 70034; 800/4KPAULS.)

FOOD AND THE SOUTHERN EXPERIENCE

We admit it. We Southerners are emotionally attached to food. We adore fixing it, eating it, and talking about it.

Food is part of our heritage of being close to the land. Food means family, too. Be it mealtime, family reunion, or funeral wakes, loved ones in Dixie still regularly convene around—what else?—food.

What's more, eating can be a religious experience for us Southlanders. Churchgoing Southerners regularly break bread together in holy communion (known down here as the "Lord's Supper"). The same goes for the more social-minded dinners on the grounds and covered-dish suppers. One feast at these gargantuan events and you'll know why even those who've never got religion have been known to get it in a hurry under such circumstances.

Our love for food goes still further, also having inspired an appetizing route to fundraising. Guess who pioneered the sale of regional cookbooks to raise money for good causes? Southern ladies, of course. What better way to round up willing donations than an all-day barbecue cookoff, fish fry, or bake sale?

For just plain fun, we can count on food to get us there. Lord only knows how many ways we celebrate food down here in Dixie. If it grows and is edible, we probably commemorate it, from the backyard watermelon repast to the countywide food festival.

ANSWERS TO "DIXIE HALL OF FAME TRIVIA TEST" ON PAGE 138.

1. Chocolate, marshmallow, caramel, and pecans. 2. Martha White Flour. 3. Pepsi-Cola. 4. President Theodore Roosevelt.

FUN WITH FOOD IN DIXIE: FESTIVALS

To see firsthand how we make our food fun, you'll need to join in the goings-on at one of our many food festivals. There's always plenty of the featured food available, but you also can count on uninterrupted entertainment. Like a themed parade (which can get pretty imaginative), a pageant to present the festival queen (if not an entire royal family), down-home music, and lots of contests (which can also get pretty inventive). Some festivals last a day and others go on for weeks at a time, but all are guaranteed to be a genuine slice of life, Southern Style.

Here's a fair sampling of how to have fun with food in Dixie (for more information, contact local chambers of commerce):

■ March

World Championship Étouffée Cook-off, Eunice, Louisiana.

Possum Creep Festival, Barnwell, South Carolina.

■ April

April

North Carolina Pickle Festival, Faison/Mount Olive, North Carolina.

World Catfish Festival, Belzoni, Mississippi. The capital of pond-raised catfish commemorates the state's premier export.

Jambalaya Jamboree, Baton Rouge, Louisiana.

World Grits Festival, St. George, South Carolina.

World's Biggest Fish Fry, Paris, Tennessee. More than eight tons of fresh Tennessee River catfish are fried up for this event.

Spinach Festival, Alma, Arkansas.

■ May

Vidalia Onion Festival, Vidalia, Georgia.

International Bar-B-Q Festival, Owensboro, Kentucky. Claimed to be the barbecue capital of the world, more than 40,000 fans join the annual feast, which features music.

Crawfish Festival, Dermott, Arkansas.

International Barbecue Festival, Memphis, Tennessee. Memphis claims to be the pork barbecue capital of the world. The more than 100,000 fans attending annually are, no doubt, practicing believers.

Cosby Ramp Festival, Cosby, Tennessee. In celebration of the "sweetest tasting, vilest smelling plant that grows."

Praline Festival, Houma, Louisiana.

■ June

Pink Tomato Festival, Warren, Arkansas. Celebrate the June harvest of tomatoes picked in the pink of their prime.

Poke Sallet Festival, Harlan, Kentucky. In honor of the wild-growing green.

■ July

South Carolina Peach Festival, Gaffney, South Carolina.

Grand Bay Watermelon Festival, Grand Bay, Alabama. Claims to be the world's largest celebration of watermelon.

Louisiana Watermelon Festival, Farmerville, Louisiana.

■ August

Watermelon Festival, Hope, Arkansas. Hope doesn't claim to have the world's largest watermelon celebration, merely the world's largest watermelons.

Strange Seafood Exhibit, Beaufort, North Carolina. Your chance to sample many exotica of the sea, thanks to the North Carolina Maritime Museum.

■ September

International Banana Festival, Fulton, Kentucky, and South Fulton, Tennessee. These river towns used to be the nation's largest distribution stop for banana shipments. The festival features a one-ton banana pudding.

Virginia Peanut Festival, Emporia, Virginia.

Turkey Festival, Raeford, North Carolina.

World Chicken Festival, London, Kentucky. Lots of "eggs-citement" at the home of Colonel Sanders' first KFC restaurant.

Apple Festival, Hendersonville, South Carolina.

Sugar Cane Festival, New Iberia, Louisiana.

Sorghum Sopping Days, Waldo, Alabama. Sop all the sorghum you crave; homemade biscuits are at the ready.

Bayou Food Festival, Lafayette, Louisiana. Submerge yourself in a plethora of Cajun specialties for a mere pittance. Part of the annual Festival Acadiens.

■ October

Okra Strut, Irmo, South Carolina. The pod of the gods is feted in fine fashion. Don't miss the Shoot-out at the OKra Corral, Irmo's celebrity okra-eating contest.

Arkansas Rice Festival, Weiner, Arkansas.

National Pecan Festival, Albany, Georgia.

National Peanut Festival, Dothan, Alabama. Its two-and-one-half mile parade is capped off with a cement mixer that spews peanuts to cheering onlookers.

Sweet Potato Festival, Tuskeegee, Alabama.

National Pumpkin Festival, Spring Hope, North Carolina.

Big Pig Jig Barbeque Cookoff, Vienna, Georgia. Festivities include a five-K "hog jog," a hog-calling competition, and a greased pig contest.

Moonshine Festival, Dawsonville, Georgia.

Kentucky Apple Festival, Paintsville, Kentucky.

Yambilee, Opelousas, Louisiana. A big (200,000 festival-goers) celebration, yam-packed with events.

Trigg County Country Ham Festival and Fair, Cadiz, Kentucky. These folks are long renowned for their country hams. Includes the world's largest country ham biscuit.

National Shrimp Festival, Gulf Shores, Alabama.

Andouille Festival, LaPlace, Louisiana.

Collard Festival, Gaston, South Carolina.

■ **November**

Chitlin Strut, Salley, South Carolina. All you care to eat of those famous fried entrails (more than 20,000 pounds to choose from).

Swine Time Festival, Climax, Georgia. As often said, feel free to make a pig of yourself here. There's even a best-dressed pig contest.

HOW TO EAT A WATERMELON SOUTHERN STYLE

■ **Selection Tips**

Best Method: Go to your garden and select a perfectly ripe *Citrullus Vulgaris.* If neither you nor your invited guests grow your own watermelons, then beg, plead, or cajole one from a neighbor or family member who does.

Next Best Method: If you come up empty-handed, head for the neighborhood produce truck or farmers' market for your watermelon.

Last Ditch Method: Should still none of the above options pan out, you will have to settle for a melon from the grocery store (in most cases, this will still be better than no melon at all). However, if you buy a storebought melon, do not attempt to pass off your melon as homegrown. Few Southerners will fall for such a ruse.

All-Method Thump Test: To select a truly ripe and juicy melon, most melon connoisseurs employ the Thump Test. A watermelon that is ready to enjoy will sound full and deep in tone when you give it a hard thump with your finger. Contrarians avow instead that the only reliable test is to press the soft end of the melon opposite the navel. When it yields to pressure, get out the napkins.

■ **Preparation Tips**

Where to Eat: A genuine watermelon repast must be conducted out-of-doors, in the yard or on the porch. Of course it will be as hot as the blue blazes outside, and humid, too, but this is as it should be. Situate everybody in a shady spot on lawn chairs, swings, and picnic tables.

What to Wear: Be sure to keep the whole affair downhome and relaxed. Bare feet encouraged. No dress-up allowed, since this can get pretty sloppy.

Who Participates: Your family, friends, and neighbors must be in attendance. Children and pets should chase about while grownups swat at gnats and catch up on the latest developments (that is, gossip). Invite the preacher and his wife, if you've a mind to.

Making Ready: Set out the watermelon(s), salt shaker, and plenty of napkins on a table. Designate an adult to cut the watermelon with a long butcher knife when everyone's ready to eat.

To cut, slice the melon in half vertically. Cut these halves like a loaf of bread, into slices about three inches thick. Cut these rounds in half.

■ How to Eat the Thing

1. Resist any urges to use a knife and fork. Not only are they unwieldly to use on a slice of seed-riddled watermelon, utensils give an aura of pretension to what is otherwise a very playful occasion. Rest assured, you don't need anything but your hands and your mouth to eat all the watermelon your heart desires and enjoy every bite.

2. Take a slice in both hands and eat it like a big cookie. Slurp, smack, lick, and savor the sweet, red meat.

3. If the juice dribbles down your chin, don't worry. Just wipe it off with the back of your hand.

4. When you encounter watermelon seeds, for heaven's sake, do not eat them. Merely spit them out on the ground and be done with them, un-less you wish to compete in a watermelon seed-spitting contest with fellow eaters. (This little game is self-explanatory. Have fun.)

5. Once you have consumed every morsel of the red flesh, toss the rind in a pile with other rinds (use them for compost). Go back for another piece and have at it again.

■ How City Folk Eat Watermelon

Directions:

1. In your kitchen, cut open a ripe watermelon. Scoop out the red flesh with a melon baller and place the balls in a mixing bowl. Avoid all seeds.

2. After you have scooped out oodles of little red balls, toss them with freshly made poppy seed dressing. Cover and refrigerate.

3. Throw the rind and seeds in the trash compactor.

4. Serve the watermelon at brunch in cute glass bowls or in individual crystal goblets. Garnish with a sprig of mint, if desired. Also makes a delightful dessert for an outdoor picnic (symphony in the park, Shakespeare under the stars, and so forth).

CHAPTER SEVEN

In God We Trust in Dixie

Fundamental Revelations That Offer a Prayer of a Chance for Understanding Dixie

Verily, verily, until ye have seen the light about religion Down South, ye cannot completely understand the Southland. Yea, it would be easier for a camel to go through the eye of a needle.

Everywhere you turn in Dixie, you can see the legacy of our religious heritage in action. It runs deep and wide in the southern culture and psyche. You won't need a divine revelation to discover that our approach to religion is one-of-a-kind. Like just about everything else Down South, we do religion *our* way and in a *big* way.

You can't really escape religion Down South. You couldn't if you tried. To put it in the terms of common Bible Belt wisdom, "You can't run from God" when you live around these parts. The upshot of all this is that if you care to truly fathom Southern Style, we advise you to factor in the kinds of godly considerations we'll be pointing out in this chapter.

YOU GOTTA HAVE RELIGION

While folks in other cultures may find it sufficient to *practice* their religion, in the Southland you've got to *have* religion.

The vast majority of Southerners know what it means to have religion. Many got religion at an early age. Some got religion, but then lost it. Still others lost their religion, but later recovered it. And some are still holding out.

Having religion is the southern way of saying you've gone whole hog for Jesus. It means you have been saved (also known as having "found the Lord"). To have been saved supplies you with a sort of holy insurance policy against spending forever in hell. (Details available for How to Be Saved, Southern Style, at most Protestant churches and all Fundamentalist ones.)

Once you have your own policy, you no longer have to worry about the dismal prospects of eternal damnation and hellfire. You've been saved from that. Instead, you can look forward to a happy and heavenly ever after, because now you've got religion. As for life on this earth, those who have been saved must live like loyal followers of Jesus (see below) and persuade those who don't have religion to get it right away.

■ Fundamentally Speaking . . .

A great many Southerners who have religion (have been saved) consider themselves "Fundamentalists." A Fundamentalist is a very conservative kind of Protestant who very carefully lives by the Book (the Good Book, that is), especially the New Testament, *to the letter.* You could very well say that the Good Book is the Fundamentalists' ultimate handbook to life. Word for word.

The standard Fundamentalist approach to religion is all the way or nothing. You can't relegate it to an hour's worship on Sunday mornings. You have to *live* it, literally by the rules of the Book, twenty-four hours a day. This is known as "practicing what you preach."

Even for Fundamentalists, how exactly to live by the Book to the letter depends upon who's reading it. This explains the proliferation of denominations of Fundamentalist faiths, such as Baptists, Methodists, Assemblies of God, Churches of God, Holiness, Pentecostals, and so forth. This also explains why there are at least fifteen kinds of Baptists, almost as many kinds of Pentecostals, and about ten kinds of Methodists. Clearly, for Fundamentalists, having religion varies six ways to Sunday and back again.

HOW THOSE WHO HAVE RELIGION TOE THE LINE

Do's:

- Praying and reading the Bible daily
- Living a godly life (setting a Christian example)
- Sharing the gospel
- Obeying the Ten Commandments
- Attending Sunday school and church services faithfully, on Sunday and during the week
- Tithing
- Teaching a Bible class
- Being on a church committee
- Being a deacon/elder/lay reader
- Singing in the choir or assisting in the nursery during church services
- Having the pastor and wife over at least once a year
- Giving to special church fund drives (building, missionary)
- Helping the less fortunate

Don'ts:

- Acting un-Christian
- Disobeying the Ten Commandments
- Neglecting your church responsibilities
- Changing church denominations
- Cussing
- Behaving rudely
- Being selfish or unforgiving
- Messing around if you're married
- Messing around if you're unmarried
- Engaging in ungodly pastimes (gambling, drinking, drugs, smoking, dancing, etc.) or consorting with those who do
- Dressing immodestly

Hardcore Don'ts:

Reading secular books (especially trashy novels, books about evolution, or similar "humanistic" topics), playing cards, attending the movies, listening to secular music, or wearing "worldly," that is, suggestive or trendy clothing.

BIG REASONS FOR TAKING RELIGION SO SERIOUSLY IN DIXIE

You are probably of the opinion that Southlanders tend to take our religion very seriously. You are right, brothers and sisters. Religion, Southern Style, is no laughing matter. Whatever your religious persuasion, it's advisable to treat the subject like the sacred southern institution it is.

Unless you are prepared for a heated and protracted argument, it is also advisable to do the following should the subject of religion Down South come up. Don't make jokes about it, don't disparage it, and don't toss out provocative statements (for instance, "Creationism is an obsolete concept"). If you do, be prepared to miss supper. Theological debates have been known to run for decades Down South, and there is little reason to believe that yours will be exempt.

Consider the reasons why.

■ Big consequences

Remember, the stakes aren't just high, according to those of us who have religion. They're high heaven, and eternal. With the surety of ever-lasting hell as the alternative, this puts having religion and spreading it in the realm of the utmost, the ulti-mate, and the urgent for its believers.

■ Big image

H. L. Mencken, man of letters, didn't dub our region the "Bible Belt" on a whim. The shoe fit earlier this century when he bestowed it; it fit a hundred years earlier; and it still fits.

Everybody knows it, too, because we've never tried to hide it. The South's You-Gotta-Have-Religion philosophy has been proclaimed to all four corners of the earth. This stance has become part and parcel of the southern identity, which means that impugning our prevalent forms of faith is tantamount to impugning Dixie.

■ Big impact

Those do's and don'ts of religion our way have wielded considerable influence on the shaping of southern culture. How else could we have developed our trademark propriety and deportment than from a legacy of Sunday school lessons and church sermons? Those essential southern virtues such as humility, kindness, and good manners do not occur in nature, even in home soil.

■ Big numbers

By sheer size alone, the Southland's body of believers is a force to be reckoned with. There are *millions* of folks who have religion Down South. Our two largest denominations, Southern Baptists and United Methodists, together have about twenty-five million members, the majority of whom live in Dixie. Add in the dozens of other denominations and sects who more or less share the same theological hymn-book, and you are looking at numbers that count for the goodly portion of Southlanders. Period.

TIPS FOR HYPOCRITES

You know who you are. Once upon a time, you had religion but let it lapse. Not that you're against having religion in principle (few Southerners take such a stand), it's just that you're content with small doses of it on an occasional basis.

Problem is, that's not enough for those around here who have religion. This means two things: (1) You've become classified as a "backslider," "fence-straddler," or "hypocrite"; (2) Unless you wish to remain in an abysmal state of grace with your more exemplary family, friends, and relations, you're going to have to make some concessions. So here are a few tried-and-true tips for hypocrites:

■ **Occasionally attend church.**

Holy day services like Easter and Christmas are popular choices, but you will want to avoid attending Sunday school or other small groups where your feet might get held to the fire for your lax behavior. This is known as the "better than nothing" technique. While in church do these things:

- Sit among the back rows of the congregation.
- Put one dollar in the offering plate when it passes and smile beautifully.
- Refrain from sleeping during the sermon. Instead, look attentively at the preacher while thinking about what you'll do when church is over.
- Be sure to exit through the front door to shake the preacher's hand. Tell him how much you enjoyed the sermon.

■ **Leave a large Bible out on the coffee table.**

Give it a place of honor in your living room, right next to your favorite magazines and the *Ideals* keepsake books. This gives the impression that you have your priorities right.

■ **Indulge in your chosen vices on the sly.**

If you are found out, stay calm. Admit your human frailty and act contrite until the lapses of another backslider become the focus of attention (which will eventually occur). Be extra discreet upon resuming your indulgences. You're under the watchful eyes of your concerned brethren and sisters.

THE RISE AND SWELL OF
THE BIBLE BELT

Believe it or not, the South hasn't always been as intent upon walking in the footsteps of Jesus as it is now. Fact is, the Southland itself didn't truly get religion in the southern sense of the word until the mid-1700s. This was because few rural settlers owned Bibles (or could read them), much less had churches to attend. It took a religious movement called the Great Awakening sweeping across Dixie to instigate our conversion. Under the impassioned exhortations of traveling evangelists, circuit riders, and farmer-preachers (often at large gatherings known as "revivals" and "camp meetings"), thousands of slumbering sinners in the South were aroused and saved from the clutches of the devil.

On the whole, Southerners took to the Great Awakening like a duck on a June bug. In contrast to their rather staid and disciplined everyday life, our forebears carried on aplenty in revivals and camp meetings. Historical accounts vouch that these events reached a pitch of unbridled emotional and physical spectacle that most Southerners would today find way out of hand. But for about 100 years, such spells of spirit-filled fervor were the accepted demonstrations of one's conversion from sin.

■ **Bodily Exercises: Letting the Spirit Move During the Great Awakening**

Falling—collapsing in a dead faint
Jerking ("taking the jerks")—convulsive head twitching
Speaking in Tongues—spontaneous speaking in languages unknown to the talker
Rolling
Running
Barking
Laughing
Trances
Visions

THE SEVEN DEADLY SINS IN DIXIE

Secularism
Not attending church regularly
Not tithing
Disparaging the South
Hubris
Bad manners
Indiscretion with your moral lapses

Let-loose worship of this magnitude is, by and large, out of vogue these days Down South as most Southerners prefer to keep their expressions of religion within current boundaries of good taste. Although some religious gatherings are prone to get somewhat unrestrained at times, they're fairly orthodox compared with the goings-on of revivalism. But if you seek, you can still find the holy-rolling venues of old-time, stoked-up, get-down religious fervor, a slice of southern history neither gone nor forgotten.

CANE RIDGE: THE SOUTH'S GRANDEST CAMP MEETING

More than 20,000 Southerners came from hundreds of miles around to Cane Ridge in Bourbon County, Kentucky, in early August 1801. Camping in tents, covered wagons, sheds, and clearings, they came to participate in a marathon of religious rallying: nonstop sermonizing, hymn singing, praying, river baptisms, marching processions, and unrestrained outpourings of spiritual fervor.

The Cane Ridge camp meeting could rightly be described as a religious extravaganza. Preachers and circuit riders addressed the camp "tabernacles," vehemently stoking the fires of repentance and zeal among the attending throngs. Issuing impassioned, vivid oratory about the terrifying torments of hell and the heavenly rewards of salvation, these sons of thunder led their worshipers to frenzied crescendos of spiritual ecstasy.

Overcome with emotion and religious conviction, members of the audiences would shriek and shout, weep, wail and mourn, and often succumb to the uncontrollable paroxysms of religious exercises (it's well documented that more than 3,000 at Cane Ridge "fell"). History also tells us that some of those in attendance were also overcome with passions that were something other than godly, resulting from sharing close quarters and a let-your-guard-down abandon. This prompted several critics of the day to observe that more souls were conceived than saved at Cane Ridge.

Camp meetings like Cane Ridge weren't confined to the Southland but were most numerous inside it. To this day you can find camp meetings (usually in early autumn) in Dixie. These versions are generally more reserved than those of the Cane Ridge era. You can expect that the preaching and singing and testifying will get pretty enthusiastic, but the more sensational dimensions of yesteryear are usually the province of isolated and backwoods assemblies.

MAKING A JOYFUL NOISE IN DIXIE

We Southerners take our religion seriously, but being an expressive lot, we're frequently disposed to doing so with a smile on our faces, a song on our lips, and often a host of expressions that are anything but staid. For us, freedom of expression demonstrably goes hand in hand with freedom of religion, and we have been known to take full advantage of these rights when the spirit moves us.

However, how to praise the Lord in Dixie is about as open to interpretation as the Holy Scriptures and can be equally as controversial from one sanctuary to the next. About the only generalization you can make is, the less orthodox the service, the more folks will participate and express themselves.

But don't let that deter you from paying a visit to a church service Down South. As any Southlander who has religion will assert, you can't afford to miss it. Instead, keep reading, then try it yourself next Sunday.

■ Making Heavenly Music on Earth

The presence of music in church services is by no means original to the Southland, but the way we have long gone about singing our heavenly praises most certainly is. Ever since the fires of revivalism blazed during the Great Awakening, Southerners have been pulling out all the stops to praise the Lord in song.

In fact, much of our region's musical tradition was cradled within the walls of southern churches. Consider-

ing how much time Southerners spend in church and considering the source of inspiration, this is perfectly understandable.

A few verses of a somber hymn or two would never do for most southern congregations. What these folk yearn for are the spirit-stirring anthems, harmonizing hymns, and toe-tapping choruses of Old Time Religion.

And the more, the better. Because not only does the music provide a sanctioned outlet for releasing spiritual zeal, the experienced know well that even if you can't count on the sermon to move you, the music assuredly will.

■ Long-Lived Bible Belt Hymns

Praise and Adoration

"All Hail the Power of Jesus' Name"
"Glorious Things of Thee Are Spoken"
"Come, Thou Long-Expected Jesus"
"Rejoice, Ye Pure in Heart"
"Crown Him with Many Crowns"
"Holy, Holy, Holy"
"Come, Thou Almighty King"
"O For a Thousand Tongues to Sing"

Faith

"Love Divine, All Loves Excelling"
"What a Friend We Have in Jesus"
"We're Marching to Zion"
"How Firm a Foundation"
"The Unclouded Day"
"The Solid Rock"
"Have Faith in God"
"Standing on the Promises"

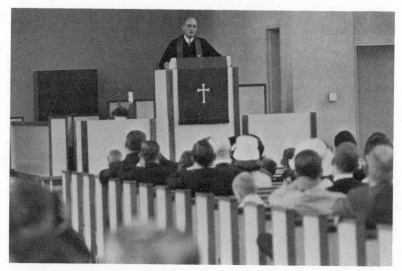

Sunday morning across the Southland, rain or shine

Repentance, Unworthiness
"When I Survey the Wondrous Cross"
"Alas, and Did My Savior Bleed"
"Jesus, Lover of My Soul"
"There Is a Fountain"
"I Am Thine, O Lord"
"Savior, Like a Shepherd Lead Us"

Salvation
"Softly and Tenderly"
"Wherever He Leads, I'll Go"
"His Way with Thee"
"I Surrender All"
"Jesus Is Calling"
"Trust and Obey"
"Nothing But the Blood"

Favorite Old-Time Religion Songs
"The Old Rugged Cross"
"Sweeter Than the Day Before"
"Rescue the Perishing"
"Shall We Gather at the River"
"Amazing Grace"

"Bringing in the Sheaves"
"Send the Light"
"Sweet By and By"
"Rock of Ages"
"When They Ring the Golden Bells"

Most dreaded hymn
"Just As I Am" (all six verses)

■ **Showing Musical Savvy in the Church Service**

Use these tips to enhance your worship wherewithal.

1. *Sing from the heart:* Make a joyful noise, even if you're tone deaf. Whether you can carry a tune is beside the point, so open up and sing like there's no tomorrow.

2. *Harmonize if you can:* Four-part singing is a favorite. Sounds pretty, too.

155

3. *Watch the song leader:* If you don't, you can never be sure when to stand or remain seated, skip a verse, or sing the Amen at the end.

4. *Demonstrate your enthusiasm:* Feel free to pat your foot or nod your head to the music. Some congregations clap to the music; others even sing responses on cue.

5. *Don't be overwhelmed by lots of bells and whistles:* Prepare yourself for something beyond a mere pipe organ should you attend a large evangelical church. Expect similarly large musical statements like eighty-member choirs, ten-piece orchestras, guitars, percussion, spotlights, and full amplification.

6. *Be especially reverent during the closing hymn (the "invitation"):* This is the chance for those who don't have religion to get it, so keep as quiet as a church mouse.

. . . But once the church service is over, don't think that the music has been silenced. One of the most rousing experiences in religious musicdom is a down-South hymnfest or gospel musicfest, enraptured choruses on earth the likes of which you've probably never heard before. Folks come from all around to appreciate or participate in these churchwide, citywide, or statewide musical convocations.

. . . *And the Eat-Your-Pious-Words Award* goes to the hymnal revision committee of the United Methodist Church, who in 1986 raised the dander of thousands of disgruntled Wesleyans by recommending the removal of the old standard, "Onward Christian Soldiers," from a forthcoming edition. Their rationale: the hymn's "unrelenting use of military images."

After a flood of indignant protests, the committee relented and decided to keep the misunderstood hymn, conceding that the lyrics referred not to overzealous militarism, but to the perpetual struggle between good and evil.

■ Emoting: Exponential Religious Expression

In many church services Down South, all that joyous singing may not be sufficient to express your religious convictions. Maybe you feel impelled to deliver a resounding Amen! after a particularly inspiring performance by the choir or upon hearing a particularly inspiring comment by the preacher. Or you may feel that you need to say a few things yourself about the matter by "testifying," or, "giving testimony" to the congregation. Perhaps you even feel led to react spontaneously and uninhibitedly as the spirit moves you, letting your body talk and your mouth speak whether you know what you're doing or saying, all in the name of the Lord.

Whatever the extent of your urgings, you can find ample company Down South, because emoting comes with the religious territory. Every congregation has its own firm persuasion regarding whether to emote and how to go about it properly, so do keep

(continued on page 158)

SHAPED NOTE MUSIC: DEEP SOUTH MUSICAL TRADITION

With its distinctive musical style, Elizabethan origins, and its poetic, narrative lyrics, shaped note music is a moving example of southern folk music.

The debt of this sonorous legacy is owed to South Carolina native Benjamin Franklin White, the first to assemble a collection of shaped note hymns. His songbook, *Sacred Harp*, put harmonizing song within the reaches of rural and frontier Southerners during the mid-1800s. The key was a simplified system of musical instruction that employed four musical syllables (fa, sol, la, mi), each of which was depicted with a shaped note (triangle, circle, square, and diamond). With no instrumental accompaniment needed, shaped note singing soon became a popular southern phenomenon, both in and out of churches.

Because of its unusual style, shaped note music has an unusual sound by traditional standards, one that's been likened to the eerie, minor-key effect of bagpipes. The lyrics are from the heart, often spinning out mournful sentiments of the common man (despair, fear, death) and religious themes (afterlife)

Shaped note singing still flourishes in today's Southland. Conventions of Sacred Harp and Christian Harmony enthusiasts often meet, and singing schools continue to instruct this unique, intriguing musical legacy.

your navigational skills sharpened.

For many, emoting is limited to an occasional and fairly conventional "Amen, Brother" (or perhaps a composed "Praise the Lord!"). For others, emoting is an authenticating dimension of their religious experience, a rite of passage of sorts into spiritual adulthood. These folk, known as Pentecostals or "charismatics," call this "getting filled with the Holy Spirit," which manifests itself in all sorts of dramatic "gifts" (most widely known are "speaking in tongues" and healing).

Then there are Southlanders whose idea of emoting eclipses the prevailing notions of modern worship. For them, exhibits of their faith include—at the least—the physical exercises of revivalism and—at the utmost—close-to-the-edge encounters with snakes and poisons.

Depending upon your religious temperaments, emoting can be either an uplifting or a disturbing experience. So before you decide to darken the door of a church Down South, you had better determine its emotive protocol. (Refer to "Worship, Southern Style," following, for tips.) Otherwise you may find yourself the proverbial fish out of water—just as you may well also find your reception to be something less than warm hearted, open armed, or open minded.

■ **Bible Belt Lexicon**

Amen corner: group of church brethren who sit in the front of the congregation and loudly issue amens and other praise words. The more they like what the preacher says, the more the amens.

Backslider: someone who once had religion but gave in to sin and lost it. Often describes one considered a repeat offender.

Bible thumper: slang for a dogmatic and proselytizing Fundamentalist.

Fundamentalists: Protestants who define five basic doctrines considered fundamental to their theology, including viewing the Bible as inerrant and therefore to be taken at its literal word, the Virgin Birth, bodily resurrection, substitutionary atonement, and second coming of Jesus.

Glossolalia: speaking in tongues; viewed by Pentecostalists and charismatics as a gift of the Holy Spirit. Few of those who speak in tongues understand what they are saying but, blessedly, others receive the gift of interpretation.

Holy Roller: slang for an overly zealous or fanatical Bible thumper. Inspired by extremists who actually roll about during moments of frenzied worship.

Mourner's bench: in old-time religion meetings, gathering place for worshipers to "pray out" the devil and "pray through" the Holy Spirit. Site of much weeping and wailing and gnashing of teeth, also of hosannas and hallelujahs.

Pentecostals: Fundamentalists who believe that one must repeatedly experience the "second blessing" of the Holy Spirit (glossolalia, healing, visions, and so forth) in order to authenticate their faith.

Revival: special series of church services with emphasis upon soul saving. Often features a visiting evangelist.

Second Coming: describes the anticipated return to earth by Jesus Christ. What everyone who has religion looks forward to.

Tent meeting: a twentieth-century version of an old-time camp meeting. Usually conducted in a temporary shelter by a traveling evangelist.

Testify: to stand before a group of worshipers and proclaim one's religious convictions or concerns.

Tithing: process of pledging and giving 10 percent of one's income (that's gross income, mind you) to church or religious causes.

Vacation Bible School: summertime church camp for school-age kids. Five or more weekday mornings of Sunday school, revival, and play school, combined.

Witnessing: process by which those who have religion tell those who don't have it why they need it and how to get it.

WORSHIP SOUTHERN STYLE: WHAT TO

TYPE OF CHURCH	CLUES AND CUES
	Minister
Staid/Orthodox (Presbyterian, Episcopal)	• Is composed, dignified. • Usually well educated (private university and divinity school). • Rarely gets emotional during sermon. • Wears vestments; looks distinguished.
Fundamentalist (Baptist, Methodist)	• Is composed but informal and friendly. • Probably went to seminary. • Will get emotional during delivery of sermon. May shout, wave arms and Bible, beat pulpit for emphasis. • Prefers to wear three-piece suits in muted colors (may remove jacket during throes of sermon).
Pentecostal (Church of God, Assemblies of God, Holiness)	• Informal, intense, and expressive. • Possibly went to seminary. • Can get very emotional during service. Gestures freely and dramatically. Will shout, beat pulpit, strut amongst congregation. May preach for hours. • Will probably "lay on hands" for healing and other gifts of the Spirit. • Often preaches in shirt-sleeves. Looks undistinguished, intentionally.
Extremists/Holy Rollers	• Neither sophisticated nor erudite but doesn't pretend to be. • Employs fanatical style: prolonged and histrionic oratory, no holds barred. • Conducts congregations to pitches of frenzy. • Directs "acts of faith" (snake handling, strychnine ingestion, etc.) of congregation.

EXPECT IN A CHURCH SERVICE IN DIXIE

Congregation	Other Denominal Distinctions
• Same. • Uses Bibles in pew racks. • Except for responses and hymns, keeps quiet. • Distinguished folk, fairly cosmopolitan.	• Baptizes infants with a sprinkle of holy water. • Refer to the Eucharist as Holy Communion. • Urban, suburban, and sometimes small-town. • Doesn't oppose a nip or two of libations.
• Same. • Brings own Bibles to church. • Usually reserved, but can be responsive. May issue spontaneous amens or clap after stirring music. May weep during closing hymn. May profess or testify if encouraged by preacher. • Just plain folk. Conservative in appearance and attitudes.	• Baptizes adults with a dip in a pool of water. • Refers to the Eucharist as the Lord's Supper. • Found anywhere and everywhere down South. • Vehemently opposes a nip of any quantity.
• Informal, expectant and expressive. • Brings own Bible to church. • Can get very emotional during service: may wave arms and moan, pray aloud softly, speak in tongues, clap. May say amens and other praise words spontaneously. • May help "lay on hands." • Very plain folk. Ultra-conservative in appearance and attitudes.	• Baptizes adults (dunks or anoints). • Refers to the Eucharist as the Lord's Supper. • Suburban, small-town, rural. • Vehemently opposes a nip of any quantity.
• Same. • May not own a Bible or be able to read one. • Employs wide-open means of expression, no holds barred; physical exercises *en extremis*, chanting, shaking, shouting, rolling, wailing. • Demonstrates religious faith by performing death-defying acts (sometimes they work, sometimes they don't).	• No other generalizations possible, except that they are scattered across the backwoods of Dixie.

WHEN RELIGION GOES UPTOWN IN DIXIE

As we Southerners are fond of saying, there's a church on every street corner Down South. Why, we've got so many churches around here that sometimes they even outnumber the service stations. And although this may seem a trifle exaggerated to those Not From Here, those who have seen it for themselves know it's pretty close to God's truth.

Our plenitude of churches is but one of many things about Dixie religion we take for granted, like—to offer a monumental example—the southern megachurch, a fundamentalist church that often surpasses small colleges in attendance, facilities, operating budgets, and endowments. You will find at least one megachurch in every sizable southern city these days (and others yearning to be one).

Folks who don't know better could well mistake one of these massive complexes of gracious buildings and spacious grounds for a large corporation or private school. They wouldn't be far from the truth. A southern megachurch is these and more—lots more—because there's something for everyone at a megachurch. Seven days a week. Which is exactly the point.

If you belong to a megachurch (head counts usually range between 2,500–6,000), you and your fellow church-goers could take advantage of the following:

1. Attend Sunday services and Bible classes in luxurious quarters with hordes of other members. Don't let the television cameras in the sanctuary distract you; that's just the weekly broadcast in production.

2. Sing in one of the several choirs or choral groups or play in the orchestra. In the summer, travel with a touring chorus to distant locations.

3. Work out regularly at the fitness center in the "Family Life" facility. (You might want to swim some laps, play basketball, or bowl.) Take the kids there for an interchurch team basketball game.

4. Enroll your children in the church's accredited school. Have them participate in its extracurricular activities, such as drama, debate, gymnastics, and soccer.

5. Attend intensive Bible study sessions taught by renowned visiting Bible scholars and theologians.

6. Help host statewide denominational association meetings.

7. Chaperone the annual teen tour to the Holy Land.

8. Patiently explain yet again to your country cousins that your megachurch is *not* a religious country club in disguise.

TUNING IN TO JESUS DOWN SOUTH

Not only is there a church on every street corner in Dixie, there are a half dozen in every home, all as close as our television dials. And dial we do Down South, scores of us tuning in channels of blessings at all hours of the day.

Praise be to Pray-TV, from which these blessings flow. Home of the "video vicars" and their praise-and-pray corps (plus local legions of faithful armchair soldiers), Pray-TV is the next best thing to Baby Jesus Himself to a great many of us Southerners. With our Pray-TV, we need not fast for forty days and nights, much less forty seconds, for an infusion of gospel inspiration between church services (often delivered, no less, with a southern accent, Praise the Lord!). Nor do we lack for pep talks, advice, entertainment, pathos, or even real-life drama. We just need to turn on our televisions.

Here in the heartland of Pray-TV, finding Jesus on the airwaves is old hat. We've been tuning in for a helping of gospel or gospel music for generations, first on radio and later on television. Some very familiar examples include old-time religion radio stations, broadcasts of "First church" Sunday services (radio and television), and native son Billy Graham's "Hour of Decision."

Having Pray-TV in the channel lineup has put having religion in a new and different light, to say the very least. And despite the long shadows cast by certain former luminaries of the medium, Pray-TV today is as much a part of our religious landscape as Wednesday night prayer meetings.

Quite naturally, our Bible Belt is homeplace to several of Pray-TV most illustrious evangelists and empires:

Mother Angelica: From a start with Pat Robertson, this Birmingham-based Franciscan nun sends out inspirational broadcasts daily from her Eternal Word TV Network.

Jerry Falwell: He broadcasts fundamentalist services from his 21,000-member Thomas Road Baptist Church in Lynchburg, Virginia, which is also home to his Liberty University. Falwell founded the Moral Majority (later a part of his Liberty Federation) and was temporary chairman of the foundering PTL Club in 1987.

Jimmy Swaggart: His Jimmy Swaggart Ministries, including the Jimmy Swaggart Bible College, is located in Baton Rouge, Louisiana. He has two syndicated Pray-TV programs: "Jimmy Swaggart" and "A Study in the Word." He's known for his fulminating evangelistic, old-time religion style and for failing to live up to his own ideals.

Pat Robertson: Presidential aspirations aside, this disciple of the hard right and founding father of the Pray-TV format begat The 700 Club, the Christian Broadcasting Network, and CBN University (of which he is chancellor), all based in Virginia Beach, Virginia.

■ Jim and Tammy Bakker: Carpetbaggers Run Amok

Wouldn't you know it, they weren't even From Here. But like Sherman, they left a scarred swath of destruction and ill will behind them, all for a cause that not even most Bible Belters can justify.

What it all boils down to is that Jim and Tammy got too tangled up in their own britches. One does, however, have to begrudge them credit for marketing smarts, wrapping earthly aspirations in a tantalizing "name it and claim it," feel-good pop gospel of prosperity. It worked. Folks flocked to learn how they could have it all with Jesus and go first class, too. Praise the Lord!

But lo, this did not sit well with those who could not find this modern gospel in their Bibles. These people were not in the least bit happy to have the duo propounding a substitute for good, old, tried-and-true fundamentalism. Soon, all was not well in the holy land, Down South.

Then an epic commotion broke loose in 1987. Jimmy had sinned, big-time! A flap to beat all ensued. Jim and Tammy retreated. Everybody else in Pray-TV joined the fray, trading accusations and jabs in the name of Jesus. The Bible Belt was nearly torn asunder. The rest of the world forsook "Dallas" and "Dynasty" to watch the unholy wars rage.

Like Imelda and Ferdinand, the deposed couple held intermittent press conferences and searched for a new home and new horizons. Eventually Jimmy went to prison for a few years and Tammy got a makeover and a divorce.

To be continued.

TURNED OFF AND TUNED OUT IN DIXIE

Even though our Southland is home to a host of Pray-TV evangelists, don't take it on blind faith that the entire Southland is taking these fellows' words as the holy Word. Lord, no. Far from it. Many of us wouldn't give you two cents for Pray-TV— much less *to* Pray-TV—and those who consider themselves naysayers include a sizable portion of those who have religion.

But it figures, the subject being religion, that Pray-TV would become the target of some of the most unholy debates around, even were it not for some unholy aspects of its own. After all, this is the Bible Belt, land where having religion and respecting it are issues of grave consequences in both the here and hereafter and where finding theological agreement is about as likely as finding the Holy Grail. When the subject of Pray-TV comes up, you'll hear Southerners square off about these points of contention.

■ **Pray-TV is actually Pay-TV.**

Pray-TV can't fill your cup for long unless you do the same for it. If you join its loyal followers, be prepared to pay a price, usually sweetened with merchandise, boosterism ("Become a Heavenly Walk partner!"), and telethon pledge drives with dramatic pleas ("If we don't raise $10 million by Friday, this ministry will cease!").

■ **Pray-TV is McReligion.**

With its slick, variety show/telethon format, Pray-TV often amounts to little more than religious fast food (some prefer to call it junk food). In other words, a steady diet of Pray-TV may be easy to get and may go down easy, but it's better suited as a religious snack, not a square meal.

■ **Holier-than-thou holy wars.**

Things can get mighty unholy in the world of Pray-TV, what with backbiting and backstabbing amongst its competing contingents, questionable financial practices, and even behind-our-back moral turpitude. This understandably worries many followers who would prefer that the Bible Belt be a guiding light, not the laughing stock.

PRAY-TV TRIVIA TEST

1. In which southern state did televangelist Ernest ("Healll!") Angley grow up?
2. What is Tammy Faye Bakker's complete name?
3. With what publisher was Jerry Falwell involved in a libel suit?
4. Who was Pat Robertson's long-time sidekick and co-host?
5. Match these wives with their televangelist husbands: Dede, Macel, Frances.

(Answers on page 167.)

SOUTHERN STYLE #6: TELEVISION EVANGELIST AND WIFE

He's got a hotline to heaven. She's his heavenly helpmate.

In his coat pocket: brochure for his latest Bible instruction video ($39.95 to Club members), day's schedule—taping of show, speaking engagement at businessmen's luncheon, press conference (introducing line of Bible character toys), afternoon meeting with state politicos, fund-raising dinner for his Heavenly Walk College.

Signet ring with inset diamonds in cross design.

18-K gold Heavenly Walk Club logo pin.

Silently reviewing words of her upcoming solo.

Wearing makeup from her line of Heavenly Walk Beauty Products (sold at home shows by Club members).

Silk foulard tie and pocket square.

Rolex Datejust watch with diamond Bezel (gift from wealthy trustee).

18-K gold bracelet.

St. John knit dress.

Special limited edition leatherette Bible—available to dedicated supporters of The Heavenly Walk Club ($150 plus postage and handling).

Her latest book, *Pray Your Way to Heavenly Beauty* (available in bookstores; video to come soon). Folded inside book is day's agenda: tape television show, meet with book publicist, ladies' association luncheon, Club fund-raising drive strategy meeting with club officers, press conference, session with interior designer to refurbish studio reception areas, college fund-raising dinner with husband.

In his pants pockets: money clip with $340 in bills, no change (sound of jingles would be déclassé); sterling silver key ring with Club logo; keys to Jaguar XJ12 (gift of wealthy board member), five-bedroom home ("nothing special"), and office.

Custom-made three-piece suit from Paul Stuart.

Doug Mondress

Bruno Magli pumps.

Bally dress loafers.

HOW POLITICS AND RELIGION MIX IN DIXIE

Naturally, there's no such thing as the separation of church and state in the Southland. How could something like that conceivably happen in a region so aptly known as the Bible Belt? It couldn't, and it hasn't. Why, all hell could just as easily freeze over.

It should come as no surprise to learn that this connection between church and state leads, by and large, in one direction only, from church to state. When as many constituents have religion as does the South, there's not much latitude for it to be any other way. True, the Madalyn O'Hairs of the world have had it their way on momentous occasions, but they're just whistling Dixie when you get right down to it. If the Bible Belters don't approve, you might as well kiss a cause goodbye, such as:

- *Repeal of Blue Laws,* which mandate the closure of most establishments on Sundays.
- *Repeal of local liquor options,* with which counties determine by vote whether liquor can be sold/served within their limits (many remain "dry" to this day).

- *Legalization of gambling* (bingo included).
- *Use of textbooks with themes of secular humanism,* which include those scientific theories (for instance, evolution) and social attitudes (for instance, careers for women) that are believed to contradict biblical teachings.

Smart observers will notice that toeing the religious line has slackened considerably for many Southlanders in recent years. As a result, recreation in Dixie these days may include playing the lottery or racetrack as easily as playing Bible trivia, and resting on the Sabbath may entail heavy-duty shopping in the mall or a liquid lunch at the corner fern bar after church.

But don't be misled into believing that these are universally embraced choices. Many, many Southerners spend entire Sundays at church, refraining from secular influences. Still, no matter what the predominant biblical theology, forever immutable is the profound and lasting influence of religion across the Southland. Take that as gospel.

ANSWERS TO "PRAY-TV TRIVIA TEST" ON PAGE 165

1. North Carolina. 2. Tamara Faye Lavalley Bakker. 3. Larry Flynt, publisher of Hustler *magazine. 4. Ben Kinchlow. 5. Dede Robertson, Macel Falwell, Frances Swaggart.*

CHAPTER EIGHT

Good Old Boys Are Good Sports

The Other Religion of the Southland and Preferred Forms of Worship

Seems like we Southerners are happiest when we're out of doors. Put us outside in the backyard, beside the creek, tending the vegetable garden, or on the deer stand in the north forty and you'll find yourself some kind of happy Southerners. Happiness turns to ecstasy if we're outdoors *and* barefoot. The universal Good Old Boy or Gal in us will emerge, as right as rain and just as welcome.

In fact, not having a little dirt under our fingernails or on the soles of our feet—at least on occasion—is the exception because we Southerners belong to the land. Not surprisingly then, we have yet to run short of entertaining reasons to get out of doors. What nature has not already generously provided, we have ingeniously invented: a bonanza of pursuits of happiness outdoors—sports, Southern Style. It's our heritage, which means that almost all of us are country folk at heart, even the most effete residents of our New South Gothams.

This also means that once a genuine Southerner goes outside, it's Down South all the way.

THE GOD'S TRUTH ABOUT SPORTS DOWN SOUTH

Sports is major league material in Dixie. It's *big* stuff. Sports is part of the Holy Southern Trinity, along with religion and food. There is no life Down South without sports. It's that simple. And that important.

We behold our unwavering dedication to sports as a divine calling Down South, a legacy ordained by God. Many in Dixie believe that on the eighth day of creation, God created sports and it was good.

This revelation will help to explain something else significant to the subject. Southerners do not think of sports in terms of recreation. Recreation is for people who think in terms of "leisure time activities," which is only a small step away from "pastimes" and, worst yet, "hobbies." This may be fine for old folks or the housebound, but it just won't do for any self-respecting Southlander. Sports, Southern Style, demands whole-hog body-and-soul dedication. One does not dabble in sports around here, even if one cannot participate. To us:

- *Sports is tradition.* It means we can follow in our forebears' footsteps, true to Down-South style, whether it be firing a rifle or a football.

- *Sports is the good earth.* It reunites us with mother nature and our motherland. You know what that means.
- *Sports is down to earth.* Like we are.
- *Sports is a common denominator.* It's something we can all share, despite other differences.
- *Sports is fun.* And we're always a threat for a good time around here.

■ Core Sports of Dixie

Not just any old sport will do in Dixie. We definitely have our druthers about what makes for a real southern sport. No matter that the New South has arrived, endowing us with more cosmopolitan concepts in sporting. The core sports come first. Anything else, including the newcomers, are add-ons. They come later.

These are the Core Sports of Dixie:
- Football
- Football
- Football
- Basketball
- Baseball
- Hunting
- Fishing

FOOTBALL: THE OTHER RELIGION IN DIXIE

Let's get specific. Next to Jesus, the South loves football most. Like the good Lord, football occupies a very special place in Southerners' hearts. Like religion, football is something all Southlanders learn about from an early age and live with till death. It can inspire us to behave in ways not otherwise sanctioned in modern society. Utter an unkind word about either religion or football, and folks around here are liable to brand you a heretic.

Sure, we love basketball and we're mighty fond of baseball, but if we were forced to make a choice, there's no doubt about the outcome. The Southland is football land, with more fans and teams per capita than any other place in America. Come fall, anything except the bare necessities—other sports included—takes a back seat to football.

Exalted above all else is college football. Like Elvis and fried chicken, college football is a sacrosanct southern institution. Don't ask us to imagine life Down South without college football. We'd rather give up Santa Claus.

So believe us when we tell you that *nothing* can compare to the hog-wild football fanaticism that saturates the Southland each autumn and the sheer madness that erupts each weekend in our college towns. There's nothing like it. Perhaps the closest thing to it might be the gung-ho gospel fervor of a freshly converted backslider, but even we would not mislead you that such burning religious zeal can be so persistently sustained.

171

Just why is it that many Southerners would consider performing compromising acts to get 50-yard-line tickets to the Alabama-Auburn game? Why would otherwise sensible individuals happily remit usurious fees for the privilege of leasing a parking space near a college stadium? Why do some southern parents pray to be blessed with a football champion the way others pray to be blessed with the Messiah?

Lots of people Not From Here think they know why, but usually they're hopelessly misled. As a student of the South, you ought to know the difference.

WHY SOUTHERNERS ARE SO DADGUM CRAZY ABOUT FOOTBALL

All right, sports fans, let's get it straight once and for all why so many Southerners are such die-hard, dyed-in-the-wool college footballs fans. Here's the real lowdown, separating the fiction (some pretty creative stuff!) from the genuine facts.

■ Fiction

The "Forget, Hell!" theory: This notion (obviously not formulated on home turf) holds that we Southerners have built our football powerhouses and passions to exact revenge upon those damn Yankees. Obviously not formulated on reason, this theory fails to consider a few key facts, including the paucity of opportunities for blood-letting that a typical conference schedule avails. This means that we'd be making a pitifully long run for a short slide or, in most cases, no slide a'tall. Also ignored is the fact that we have more than plenty intra-Southland rivalries of our own to tend to, and neither the ethnic composition of our teams nor our fans suggest that an overwhelming urge for revenge threatens to burst loose anytime in the next millenium. So to those who offer this disingenuous position, we reply not "Forget, hell," but "Who's *really* carrying a grudge?"

The Military Metaphors theory: This is a tangential corollary to the "Forget, Hell!" notion. True, team sports in general often possess martial characteristics (plans of attack, infantry, cavalry, and artillery), but unless you are firmly convinced that Southerners are avid warmongers desperate for a sanctioned outlet, this Johnny Reb-in-helmet-and-pads theory peters out in a hurry.

The Ticket Out of Dodge theory: Be careful with this one, or you're liable to rile up more than a few Southerners. Fact is, few of our boys have sweated bullets just to hitch an all-expense-paid ride out of Dixie. On the contrary, they're just doing what their mamas and daddies raised them to do. Besides, those who make it to stardom are usually the most vociferous defenders of the Southland and have been known to sponsor a few converts along the way.

The Misplaced Priorities theory: Elitist detractors like to observe disdainfully that the South is a region with far more gumption than education and far more interest in winning championships than four-year degrees. *Au contraire.* We'll be the first to agree that we often spare no expense for our college football teams. But as every sensible southern college administrator knows, those game receipts and television rights are far more generous than the tax base in most of their states will ever be, and they'd be nuts to bite the hand that feeds them well.

■ Fact

It's democratic, it's all-American, and it's southern to boot.

Having the right stuff in this case doesn't require wealth or genius. This playing field's wide open to any Good Old Boy who's got grit and talent enough to hold his own in the trenches (not unlike becoming a country music star, you might say). Fandom knows no barriers, either, since all fans are really just Good Old Boys or Gals at heart, gathering to watch a bunch of southern folk heroes tussling it out on the gridiron.

It's a great chance to party—all fall, all over Dixie.

College football season Down South packs in all the revelry and excess of Mardi Gras for a three-month marathon (plus maybe a bowl game) without the prospects of Lenten penance—all within driving distance, too. Lest you've forgotten, we Southlanders are socializers *extraordinaire.* So what better opportunity for us to eat, drink, and be merry, nonstop? This is *football* and you're in the Dixie outdoors, by golly, and what grander excuse to party could anyone ask for?

We get to let it all hang out.

Attending a college football game Down South gives us special dispensation to cross the otherwise hard line of good deportment and decorum. Commonly known as "getting fired up" or "showing team spirit," this explains why many of us choose to look like complete fools, dressed in get-ups that have no other place in the civilized world. It's also good enough reason for us to behave like complete fools, too, hollering for all we're worth, waving our arms and jumping around like holy rollers, and similarly tampering with the limits of good taste.

We can talk to God in public.

During the course of a game, college football fans Down South frequently and openly talk with God on a first name basis, employing a broad repertoire of invocations to suit the action downfield. Making a plea for divine intervention in public is never more commonplace than during the crucial moments of a game, when multitudes of Southerners can be heard alternately beseeching "Holy #@★&! God almighty!" or "O Lord, have mercy on us *now,* let that young'un in the end zone catch the ball!"

Men are men and women aren't.

Here's one boys club that will never have to worry about admitting women, because not even a sturdy country gal from Dixie has enough brawn to make the cut for this form of hardball.

We just happen to be right good at it.

Must be all that good southern cooking and clean living in God's country, because we sure know how to grow some strapping big boys. Topped off with a generous helping of southern work ethic and pride, building formidable football teams is just one of those things we're cut out to do.

FOR THE RECORD:
NCAA CHAMPIONSHIP FOOTBALL TEAMS
FROM THE SOUTHLAND
(Division I)

Proof positive we take our football seriously.
1992 Alabama
1990 Georgia Tech (tie with Colorado)
1981 Clemson
1980 Georgia
1979 Alabama
1978 Alabama (AP Poll)
1973 Alabama (UPI Poll)
1965 Alabama (AP Poll)
1964 Alabama
1961 Alabama
1958 LSU
1957 Auburn (AP Poll)
1951 Tennessee

SOUTHERN STYLE #7: COLLEGE FOOTBALL FANS
They're pumped up and ready for a rout.

A WEEK IN THE LIFE OF A TYPICAL FAN

Down in Dixie, the game's the thing. All week long.

Sunday: Reads every word of the newspaper's Sunday sports section. Watches team's postgame show on afternoon television and the sports report on the local evening news.

Daily: Follows the scouting reports in the newspaper and on television. Analyzes prior game, top-ranked teams, conference teams, and upcoming game's opponent with fellow sports fans at the office.

Monday: Spends majority of day discussing game with pals at office. If team lost, argues how statistics prove it really won despite scoring fewer points. Late afternoon, tunes in radio for AP and *USA Today* poll results. Makes plans for next game: who's going along, who's driving, when to leave.

Tuesday: Reads new issue of *Sports Illustrated*. Glances through other sportsrags at newsstand.

Wednesday: Spends lunch at desk reading this week's batch of tip sheets. PM: plays weekly flag football game (intra-city league).

Thursday PM: Attends son's Pop Warner football game.

Friday: Places bet with football pool at office and elsewhere. May depart midday for tomorrow's game if owns motor home, or will attend local high school matchup that night.

Saturday: Rises early; scans newspaper for high school scores and any last minute news about college teams. Dresses in team colors (runs the gamut from tokenism to full dress uniform) and packs picnic (fried chicken, bloody marys, and beer, of course). Heads off to game with spouse and friends in "fan van" (conversion van in team colors), Jeep Cherokee, or the like (team mascot emblazoned on spare tire cover, rear window, "diplomat" car flags, and front tag). Arrives in college town, which is crawling with similarly attired fans in similarly decorated cars and trucks. Cheers spontaneously on street and is greeted with equally enthusiastic responses by nearby fans. Eats tailgate lunch (may even bring barbecue grill). Tours sections of campus if time permits. Enters stadium at least an hour before game time to: (1) see team walk the field and (2) get worked up into a frenzy by kickoff time. Goes wild at opening kickoff and for four quarters thereafter. Returns home on same day in sassy spirits or sore as hell.

SOUTHERN FRIED FOOTBALL

Some of the more noteworthy claims to fame of schools here in football country.

■ Best Teams

The first measure is a zero in the loss column.

Alabama, 1961: Outscored ten regular season opponents 287–22 and then beat Arkansas in the Sugar Bowl 10–3. All-SEC quarterback Pat Trammell led the offense while linebacker Lee Roy Jordan led the defense.

LSU, 1958: Led by the famous "Chinese Bandits" on defense and Heisman Trophy winner Billy Cannon on offense, Paul Dietzel's best team at LSU went 11–0, outscoring the opposition 285–53.

Georgia Tech, 1952: Bobby Dodd's best team had eight All-SEC players and went 12–0 to win the national championship. Running back Leon Hardeman led the offense, and the Morris brothers, George and Larry, led the defense.

Honorable Mention: Clemson, 1981 (12–0); Alabama, 1979 (12–0); Auburn, 1957 (10–0); Tennessee, 1938 (11–0); Georgia, 1946 (10–0); Ole Miss, 1959 (10–1).

■ Loudest Fans

Where attendance is not measured in numbers, but in decibels.

LSU: Nobody can yell like a Cajun who has had all day to get ready for the game.

Clemson: What would you expect from 75,000 people who had the nerve to wear orange overalls?

Honorable Mention: Georgia, South Carolina, Tennessee.

■ Tough Tickets

Scalpers' delights, if the scalpers can get a ticket.

Clemson–South Carolina: In the state of South Carolina, losing these is grounds for justifiable homicide.

Auburn–Alabama: A few of these spread around in the right places will get you elected governor.

Georgia–Florida: In the divorce courts of Georgia and Florida, they decide on the custody of these before the children.

■ Fight Songs

The most frequent amount of times they are played in a single game.

"Rocky Top" (Tennessee): 6,454. Would be more if the band didn't have to stop to play the national anthem.

"Glory, Glory to Old Georgia." 3,951. State law says it must be played once for every ounce of Jack Daniel's consumed.

"Dixie" (Ole Miss): 1,334. Would be more if the Rebels could score.

Honorable Mention: "Ramblin' Wreck" (Georgia Tech); "Hold That Tiger" (Clemson).

■ Best Band

No classical stuff allowed.

Virginia: Because of its often controversial skits, the "Scatter Band" is an equal-opportunity offender.

LSU: The first three notes of "Hold That Tiger" will make the hair stand up on a dead man's neck.

Tennessee: Would be No. 1 if it knew anything other than "Rocky Top."

Honorable Mention: Alabama, Clemson.

■ Best Games

Of great plays, goal line stands, and days stars were born.

LSU 7, Ole Miss 3, Halloween night, 1959: Voted the "game of the decade" by the SEC, LSU was ranked No. 1 and Ole Miss No. 2. Billy Cannon's 89-yard punt return with ten minutes left put the Tigers ahead. Ole Miss drove close to the LSU goal but was stopped on fourth and one.

Notre Dame 24, Alabama 23, Sugar Bowl, 1974: The lead changed hands six times as Notre Dame prevailed to win the national championship. After a 69-yard punt by Alabama's Greg Gantt, Notre Dame was backed up to its one-yard line with a one point lead. But the Irish gambled and won as quarterback Tom Clements hit tight end Robin Weber on the 38 to secure the victory.

Alabama 33, Ole Miss 32, Oct. 4, 1969: Quarterback Archie Manning of Ole Miss set the all-time SEC record for total offense in a single game, but it wasn't enough as Alabama and Scott Hunter won by a point. Manning had 436 yards passing and 104 yards rushing.

Honorable Mention: Georgia Tech 7, Alabama 6, 1962; Georgia–Florida (any year); North Carolina 34, North Carolina State 33, 1972; Clemson 10, North Carolina 8, 1961; Georgia 28, Georgia Tech 24, 1971.

—"Southern Fried Football" © 1986 by *The Atlanta Journal-Constitution.* Reprinted with permission.

TOUCHDOWN TRADITIONS

Match the post-touchdown spirit with its school.

1. Mascot does pushups equal to total game score.
2. Fans used to ring cowbells before visiting coach Bear Bryant had his say.
3. Fans clap politely, if at all.
4. Fires a cannon.

A. North Carolina   B. Virginia Tech   C. Duke
D. Clemson   E. Mississippi State   F. North Carolina State
(Answers on page 180.)

JAN KEMP: ACADEMIC JOAN OF ARC

Some of the most exemplary practitioners anywhere of southern hospitality have to be our football powerhouse universities. They are more than happy to supply athletes with the facilities, amenities, and services that the rest of their student bodies (and most of the free world) only dream of having, and in the spirit of our foremost football tradition, most Southerners see these perks as a fair enough trade for a winning season.

But in 1982, one lady decided to put her foot down on the unspoken perquisite of college athletics, handing passing grades to failing athletes. Jan Kemp, professor of Remedial Studies at the University of Georgia, was demoted for her contrariness. She complained and was fired.

But Jan Kemp held her ground. She sued, and the state of Georgia was thrown into a tizzy. To many, Kemp became Public Enemy Number One, but in the bitter end she was vindicated. Defying the university's athletics-first attitude, an outraged jury awarded her $1.1 million and her former job. The university lost its president and Kemp lost her husband, but precedence of sheepskins over pigskins in academia was reaffirmed.

PRO FOOTBALL: RIDDLE OF THE SOUTHLAND

Strange but lamentably true, our awesome reputation for playing ferocious football becomes a laughable one when our professional teams take the field. That the hapless Atlanta Falcons and New Orleans Saints have piddled around with this holy sport of Dixie for decades has been a big bug in the craw of Southerners everywhere. You must admit, twenty years and only two divisional championships is a long time for any fan to keep the faith, even down here in Football Country.

New Orleans Saints ™

Atlanta Falcons ™

There is a way out of this quandary, however, and it's certainly worth a try: Put the local football factories to work and put genuinely *southern* teams in uniform, 100 percent homegrown only, nobody else allowed.

Why not? Our boys are born and bred to play football to *win*. To win for mama and daddy, for their hometown, for their alma mater, and for the Southland. Lose a game and not only have these fellows tarnished their reputations, they've let everyone down for miles around. And Bubba Ray knows better than to do *that*.

Fans, too, would have plenty more motivation, what with all those home boys grueling it out on the gridiron. Like college football, they'd really have something to cheer about. Now that's a far more inspiring proposition than watching players from God-knows-where flubbing up and getting paid handsomely to do it.

Answers to "Touchdown Traditions" on page 179. 1. D; 2. E; 3. A, C, F; 4. B.

ALL HEPPED UP FOR HOOPS IN DIXIE

Not every college in Dixie succumbs to total football madness each fall, if the truth be told. At some schools around the Southland, football season is a mere waiting game for more promising activity.

A football matchup for these Southlanders makes for a pleasant fall afternoon's outing, but it is hardly cause for working up a sweat. Those in attendance are more aptly described as polite spectators than rowdy fans. Traffic jams? No problem, unless the tailgate parties get out of hand.

But just hold on. There's a good reason why these paragons of restraint choose to behave so. They are saving themselves for basketball. And for good reason: They live in the reigning kingdoms of southern basketball, where the roundball tradition runs every bit as deep and proud and successful as football at any pigskin university elsewhere. Come the opening tip-off, brace yourself, because all the frenzy of the biggest southern football schools will erupt in equally full force on the courts.

Basketball bravado like this is nowhere more entrenched than in North Carolina and Kentucky, whose college teams wield wicked clout without fail in conference and NCAA play. Their records and reputations say it all. Thanks to them, basketball in Dixie is on a roll.

This sort of mighty ball is played elsewhere in the Southland, too, at all NCAA Division levels, by male and female teams. (Every roundball fan knows about the formidable prowess of the SEC's lady basketballers.) These days basketball is no longer the stepchild sport of Dixie. It does us proud and, with the kind of court and crowd action under muster, no wonder.

NCAA CHAMPIONSHIP BASKETBALL TEAMS FROM THE SOUTH (DIVISION I)

Men's

1993 North Carolina	1951 Kentucky
1992 Duke	1949 Kentucky
1991 Duke	1948 Kentucky
1986 Louisville	
1983 North Carolina State	*Women's*
1982 North Carolina	
1980 Louisville	1991 Tennessee
1978 Kentucky	1989 Tennessee
1974 North Carolina State	1988 Louisiana Tech
1958 Kentucky	1987 Tennessee
1957 North Carolina	1985 Old Dominion
	1982 Louisiana Tech

DIXIE SPORTS HALL OF FAME

Given our divinely assigned passion for sports Down South, you might expect that we accord our sports heroes nothing less than sainthood. You'd be right. Those who become all-time sports legends receive as much honor and deference around here as Saint Paul himself, and maybe even more.

Those most blessed among men and women from the Southland include:

Muhammad Ali (Kentucky). Three-time heavyweight boxing champion.

Hank Aaron (Alabama). Baseball slugger and Hall of Famer.

Arthur Ashe (Virginia). Tennis great; Wimbledon and U.S. Singles champion.

Evelyn Ashford (Louisiana). Olympic medalist and world champion sprinter.

Paul ("Bear") Bryant (Arkansas). Invincible football coach.

Joe Lewis

Paul ("Bear") Bryant on the sideline

Tracy Caulkins (Tennessee). Olympic swimming gold medalist.

Steve Cauthen (Kentucky). Thoroughbred racing jockey.

Ty Cobb (Georgia). Baseball slugger and Hall of Famer.

Howard Cosell (North Carolina). Controversial sports commentator.

Dizzy Dean (Arkansas). Baseball pitcher and sportscaster.

Bobby Jones (Georgia). Golfing great and Grand Slam victor.

Meadowlark Lemon (North Carolina). Harlem Globetrotters star and perennial crowdpleaser.

Joe Louis (Alabama). Twelve-year heavyweight boxing champion.

Sugar Ray Leonard (North Carolina). Welterweight boxing champion (1980–82).

Willie Mays (Alabama). Baseball slugger and twice MVP.

Wilma Rudolph (second from left)

Willie McCovey (Alabama). Home run star, MVP, and Hall of Famer.

Jesse Owens (Alabama). First black Olympic track and field gold medalist.

Leroy ("Satchel") Paige (Alabama). Legendary baseball pitcher in Negro leagues and 1971 Hall of Famer.

Walter Payton (Mississippi). All-time NFL leader in yards rushing.

Richard Petty (North Carolina). NASCAR trailblazer and seven-time champion.

Eddie Robinson (Mississippi). Winningest college football coach ever.

Jackie Robinson (Georgia). Baseball MVP; first black to play in majors.

Wilma Rudolph (Tennessee). Olympic medalist, record-setting sprinter.

Fran Tarkenton (Virginia). NFL career record breaker.

Wyomia Tyus (Georgia). Set world records and earned Olympic medals in women's track.

HEAVEN ON EARTH: SPORTING
Or where to find nirvana out of doors,

	CORE SPORTS
Orderlies	• They keep up with college football and will attend a few games a year. Couples are heavily into tailgating parties with cute food. • He keeps up with basketball and baseball; he will attend decisive games (often with office buddies, using tickets from a client or supplier). She probably doesn't care to go. • He goes on hunting and/or fishing expeditions during the year, often to exotic places. • Their children may play on core sports teams at school, but likely have less *mainstream* sporting interests.
Raised Rights	• They're die-hard fans of their alma mater's (college) football and basketball teams (probably have alumni season tickets); they engineer social occasions around attending each game, no matter what the travel distance. Bowl games and conference playoffs are big must-go's. He winds down on Sundays after church by watching pro football. • Duck-hunting is a winter ritual for him and his pals; bass fishing also accounts for good weekend fun. • Their children play traditional team sports at school.
Good Old Boys and Gals	• Are dedicated followers of college football and basketball. Will tune in to all games of pet teams; will attend all those within striking distance (probably have season tickets) and raise plenty of cain while there. Religiously watch pro football on TV. • If not watching a game, he is liable to be in camouflage or waders in the Dixie backwoods or backwaters (maybe the salt waters), toting a gun (or bow) or rod 'n reel. Enjoys organized turkey shoots, coon hunts, and fishing tournaments. • Their sons play core team sports from an early age (daughters will likely play hard-core softball or basketball). Everybody takes it *extremely* seriously. It may be juvenile sport, but it *ain't* child's play.
Rednecks	• Are mildly interested in football or basketball (county high school, probably), but love to watch televised games as means to hang out and put away a twelve pack or two with their buddies in their trailer. • If not watching a game, he will be up to his ears in camo, hunting whatever's in season (or maybe what's not); may be at a fishing hole. • Redneck kids *may* play team core sports, but they're more disposed to the free-wheeling pursuits (see next column).

Good Old Boys Are Good Sports

FOR THE CLASSES IN DIXIE
Down South, subject to class distinctions.

CLASS FAVORITES

- They play tennis regularly (she plays ladies' doubles twice a week at the club; he plays there weekends). They play golf on occasion (they love to go to Pinehurst, et al., too). He may play polo during the spring and summer; they may fox hunt during the fall and winter.
- The kids will play soccer, rugby, lacrosse, and similar prep sports; may be on swim or gymnastics teams (if they need a personal coach, so much the better). Young adult Orderlies will play pool and throw darts when slumming it.
- Everybody knows how to sail and how to water ski (this is, after all, the South). Families go snow-skiing out West during the holidays.

- They enjoy golf and tennis (doubles leagues are popular), usually played on public facilities or at suburban country clubs. He jogs; she's into aerobics and may even teach them.
- They may own a HobieCat or ski boat (nothing grand). Snow skiers will converge in North Carolina for party weekends.
- Swimming and gymnastics are popular choices for the kids; ballet is also a big draw for young girls.

- They are likely ardent fans of NASCAR and will make a race annually.
- Country cousins love a good rodeo.
- Other favorites (when core sports are not in session):
  Water skiing
  Motocross, etc.
  Tractor pulls
  Skeet shooting
  Bowling (in leagues)

- Loves the down 'n dirty sports like a Good Old Boy loves football. Favorites include:
  Wrestling (male and female)
  Tractor pulls, bogging, etc.
  NASCAR
  Drag racing
  Motocross
  Racing anything motorized and on wheels
  Cock fights
  Pit bull fights
- Loves to raise hell on a lake in a cheap ski boat.
- Plays a wicked game of pool.

185

GOOD OLD BOYS AND GUNS IN DIXIE

You can bet your last can of snuff that autumn is the hands-down favorite time of year for males throughout the Southland. Come fall, they get to conduct two of the most high and holy rituals of Good Old Boydom. Not only do they get to glory in the rough and tough thrills of football, they get to become headhunters in their own right, which they do *en masse*. With fall comes hunting season in Dixie; like Christmas, it's well worth waiting for the rest of the year.

Hunting is one of those things that come with the territory Down South, like bourbon whiskey. Do not try to envision the Southland *sans* hunting. That is a hopeless cause. Imagine instead, each fall and winter, hundreds of thousands of southern males clad in camouflage and crouched on tree stands or in duck blinds in the southern outback. Also imagine thousands of trucks and three-wheelers scattered like buckshot over southern backwood roads, the muddy sentinels of two-footed, tobacco-chewing predators.

This annually comes to pass Down South because hunting is a core curriculum subject for southern menfolk. If you are a Southerner and you are male, then you know how to hunt. Chances are good that you handle your gun with the same skill and nonchalance as you would a toothpick, and just about as often.

Of course you do, because as a thin-eared boy you learned how to use a long gun, just like your daddy (who probably taught you) and your an-

Duck hunting in eastern Arkansas

cestors who settled the southern frontiers and fought in wars. Hunting is your privilege and reward for having the good fortune and sense to call Dixie home. If for no other reason, you would hunt because tradition mandates it.

This is not the only reason most men of the South go hunting every chance they get and love every minute of it. Another factor accounts for why southern men crave hunting like women and will spend more time, energy, and money than you can imagine in getting their satisfaction.

Hunting is Good Old Boyism incarnate, its hallowed province and last sacred bastion. Hunting goes with Good Old Boys like a hound dog and ticks, like fatback and turnip greens. At no other time or place can the art of being a Good Old Boy be more expertly practiced than when hunting. Never mind the New South or sex role

186

confusion; there's always hunting camp.

When a man goes hunting in Dixie, life is converted from the complicated to the simple, operating under one social code ("I'm just a downhome country boy from Dixieland"), one dress code, and one, maybe two, goals ("shoot that sucker" and "pass the bottle"). Under these circumstances, being a Good Old Boy is plenty good enough, which is precisely the point.

Remember, everybody Down South knows it is only right that a southern man be a genuine Good Old Boy at heart. He can be wealthy and urbane, and he can be president; but he should always be a Good Old Boy first and foremost. Hunting is one of the finest ways there is to revel in this southernmost state of grace.

DIXIE VARMINTS
Always in season

Possum	*Squirrel*
Coon	*Cooter (turtle)*
Armadillo	*Rabbit*

A (GOOD OLD) BOY AND HIS DOG

Good Old Boys have fixed notions about dogs. The bottom line for these fellows is, a dog isn't good for much if it isn't good for hunting. But a hunting dog is an able and honored animal. It will help you track deer and chase rabbits and other critters. It will tree coons for you. It will flush quail and retrieve ducks. With all this and giving you unconditional love, too, a good hunting dog is a thing of joy forever.

A good hunting dog can also be a thing of one-upmanship. Even midst the camaraderie of Good Old Boydom, there lingers the subtle scent of status, and its presence is most detectable around hunting dogs. Do you want to impress any serious hunter? Do you wish to make the final statement about dedicated huntsmanship?

Then do not bother with fancy trappings, like ultraexpensive guns, newfangled gear, or similar badges of conspicuous consumption (you're just a downhome Good Old Boy, not a peckerhead, remember?). Invest instead in a pedigreed bird dog, preferably a pointer, one with a bloodline as long as your arm and a name to match. This is all you need to do to say it all: This Good Old Boy don't mess around. He is *serious* about his hunting.

If—still yet—you should also wish to have the final word, too, then send your bird dog to school with a world-class trainer. Put it on the championship trail, where your canine can show its stuff in rigorous tests of bird work before the critical eyes of field trials judges. As for yourself, you now can grandly consort with other "shooting gentlemen" (mostly Good Old Boys with impressive pedigrees themselves) whose labors have elevated the lot of hunting dogs to the classy status of Thoroughbreds.

MOST FAVORITE NAME FOR A DOG IN DIXIE

Beau
(as in General Beauregard)

FAST CARS AND REDNECKS

Though they reign sovereign Down South, we wouldn't go so far as to declare that the core sports are an exclusively Dixie phenomenon. We're well aware that people outside the Southland do indeed play football, roundball, and baseball and that they know how to hunt and fish (although certainly not with the finesse and flair of a Southlander).

However, there is a sport that is pure homegrown Dixie. It's a genuinely southern-made, big-bucks, big-name sport, and it's a hair-raising, hell-raising one, at that: stock car racing, better known as NASCAR (National Association for Stock Car Auto Racing).

Stock car racing got its start as the reckless sport of Dixie's daredevil piney woods boys. Spurred on by whiskey, beer, and bets, they'd show off their get-up and gumption in souped-up family cars on backwoods stretches of sand or red clay. There wasn't much money in it, but there were plenty of revved-up thrills on the tracks and off, considering the Saturday night drinking and brawling by spectators and drivers alike.

This sort of entertainment suited everybody of redneck persuasion just fine. After all, this was *their* sport (everybody else had the presence of mind to stay away), and it fast became a ribald weekend ritual across the southern outback.

Somewhere along the stretch, the sport's founding father, Bill France, Sr., decided a little organization was in order and founded NASCAR to sanction races and give the boys a championship. Their four-wheel dueling legitimized, it wasn't long before corporate sponsors upped the ante and the media decided to recognize the South's favorite warm weather spectator sport, redneck or not.

So in the space of about forty-five years, backwoods dirt road bravado has given way to big-budget, celebrity chariot races that routinely attract 50,000 or more rowdy fans. It's still as southern redneck as the day is long (only one Yankee has ever been a NASCAR champion), but it has become plumb respectable under the auspices of NASCAR. Why, these days even folks from well-heeled neighborhoods will venture to the speedways for the big races.

You can still find the Saturday night crash-and-bash races in full swing, however. As long as we have rednecks and motorized transport, some of us will be outrunning others of us for the sheer guts and glory of it, whether in cars, on tractors, motorcycles, bogmobiles, or God knows what other kind of saddle on wheels. It's the red-blooded, redneck thing to do.

■ NASCAR'S Winningest Names

Five of those in the league of all-time champions.

Richard Petty (Randleman, North Carolina). Reclusive, seven-time NASCAR champion. Known as "King Richard," "Richard the Great." Son of NASCAR trailblazer Lee Petty and father of NASCAR contender Kyle Petty.

Dale Earnhardt (Kannapolis, North Carolina). A five-time champ and top moneymaker.

Cale Yarborough (Timmonsville, South Carolina). Three-time NASCAR champ and one of the biggest moneymakers ever on the circuit.

Darrell Waltrip (Franklin, Tennessee). Has won three NASCAR cups and top dollars on the circuit.

David Pearson (Spartanburg, South Carolina). Three-time NASCAR winner and dad of NASCAR up-and-comer Larry Pearson.

PLAYING BY THE RULES DOWN SOUTH

"**K**now thy core sports" is a cardinal rule in Dixie. Knowing your core sports assures everybody that you're a good old Southerner because you're keeping up with our national interests. You *care* about the important things, which is a statement that a punctilious Southlander really can't afford not to make, regardless of his or her social station.

There is life in Dixie beyond the core sports, however. There is, indeed: high life, low life, and more than a few strata in between where, socially speaking, some Good Old Boys (and Gals) are created more equal than others. Even for the sacred rites of southern sportsdom, it seems another cardinal rule Down South often prevails: "Know thy place."

Just what happened to all those Good Old Boys and Gals united for a common cause in Dixieland sports? Well, it depends. You see, some of us Southerners are Good Old Boys only *some* of the time (quasi-Good Old Boys), those times generally being when the core sports have commenced. Others of us, however, are Good Old Boys *all* of the time, because God made us that way, core sports or tiddlywinks notwithstanding. There *is* a difference.

This means that, once beyond the core sports, sporting for the masses Down South becomes sporting for the classes, and that makes it a whole new shootin' match, folks. So much of the time many of our Good Old Boys don't get within a country mile of one another, not even for sports.

Some rules *never* get broken Down South.

CHAPTER NINE

Where to Go for a Good Time in Dixie

A Plethora of Pastimes Across Our Fair Land

By now it should be pretty clear: There's lots to do in Dixie. No doubt this is because we happen to be downright resourceful when it comes to entertaining ourselves and anybody else within earshot. Besides diversions like pilgrimages, social whirls, foodfests, and sporting events, we're forever finding opportunities to celebrate what's great about life in the Southland.

If you're aiming for good times in Dixie, then here's a plethora of ideas to get you started (and don't forget the food festivals in chapter 6).

Where to Go for a Good Time in

ALABAMA

Annual Events

JANUARY

Senior Bowl All-Star Football Classic, Mobile.

Camellia Show, Mobile.

FEBRUARY

National Championship for Amateur Field Trial Shooting Dogs, Union Springs.

Black History Month, Tuskegee.

Mardi Gras (some years in March), Mobile.

MARCH

Rattlesnake Rodeo, Opp.

Southeastern Turkey Calling Contest, Montgomery.

Azalea Trail and Festival, Mobile.

Southeastern Livestock Exposition and World Championship Rodeo, Montgomery.

APRIL

Decorators' Show House, Birmingham.

Dauphin Island Regatta, Fairhope.

Little Britches Rodeo, Clayton.

MAY

NASCAR Winston 500 Stock Car Race, Talladega.

Sacred Harp Singing, Troy.

Southern Appalachian Dulcimer Festival, Tannehill State Park.

Rhododendron Festival, Mentone.

JUNE

Helen Keller Festival, Tuscumbia.

Blessing of the Fleet, Bayou La Batre.

Hank Williams Memorial Celebration, Evergreen.

Chamber Music Festival, Guntersville.

JULY

Alabama Deep Sea Fishing Rodeo, Dauphin Island.

World Championship Domino Tournament, Andalusia.

NASCAR 500 Stock Car Race, Talladega.

AUGUST

Armadillo Round-up, Red Level.

Kudzu Festival, Birmingham.

W. C. Handy Music Festival, Florence.

Cherokee Pow-Wow, Gadsden.

SEPTEMBER

Contemporary Art Biennial (even-numbered years), Montgomery.

Racking Horse World Celebration, Decatur.

Old Courthouse Country Fair, Seale.

OCTOBER

Tennessee Valley Old Time Fiddler's Festival, Athens.

Covered Bridge Festival, Oneonta.

Alabama Tale-telling Festival, Selma.

State Fair, Birmingham.

Steam Train Fall Excursion, Huntsville.

NOVEMBER

Southern Wildlife Festival, Decatur.

Poarch Band of Creek Indians Thanksgiving Day Pow Wow, Atmore.

Championship Charity Horse Show, Montgomery.

DECEMBER

SEC Football Championship, Birmingham.

Blue-Gray All-Star Football Classic, Montgomery.

194

NOT TO BE MISSED

An eclectic selection of Alabama attractions

■ **Honor musical legends in country music** with visits to the homeplace of W. C. Handy in Florence and Hank Williams's gravesite in Montgomery.

■ **Take a covered bridge trek** across Blount County and examine four of the nation's most impressive examples of covered bridges.

■ **Enter the Space Age** at the U.S. Space Academy in Huntsville. Experience firsthand astronaut training, shuttle mission simulations, and flight crew assignments. The less intrepid can confine their explorations to the museum of space travel at the NASA Space and Rocket Center.

■ **See 150 million years' worth of geologic history** exposed in the side of Red Mountain in Birmingham. Study the Red Mountain Museum's intriguing collection of fossils and view the sun's surface through its spectrohelioscope.

■ **Pay your respects to prized coonhounds** at the Key Underwood Coon Dog Memorial Graveyard near Tuscumbia.

■ **Watch classical and contemporary performances** by an acclaimed repertory company at the Alabama Shakespeare Festival in Montgomery. Attend preshow and postshow discussions to expand your theatrical erudition.

■ **Explore the pentagonal brick forts** that formerly protected opposite ends of Mobile Bay—Forts

U.S. Space Academy

Morgan and Gaines—and review their critical roles during the War Between the States.

■ **Go fishing for lunkers** at the big bass capital of the world, Lake Eufaula.

■ **Visit two important cradles of history** within a two-block area in Montgomery: the first White House of the Confederacy, where President Jefferson Davis resided, and Dexter Avenue King Memorial Baptist Church, where, less than a century later, Martin Luther King, Jr., presided over the civil rights movement.

■ **Gather ye knowledge about important contributions by African-American trailblazers** at Tuskegee Institute National Historic Site. Visit the Carver Museum, which documents the agricultural experiments of George Washington Carver, and the Oaks, Victorian home of educator Booker T. Washington.

■ **Surround yourself with breathtaking blooming color** with a late March/early April trip to Bellingrath Gardens and Home near Mobile. Witness the beauty of 200,000 azaleas in vivid bloom in the sixty-five-acre garden of this famous estate.

■ **Learn the macabre yet fascinating facts about chemical warfare** at the U.S. Army Chemical Corps Museum near Anniston. On exhibit are more than 4,000 chemical warfare artifacts from biblical times to the nuclear age.

■ **Tour the eerie and beautiful onyx caves** of DeSoto Caverns near Childersburg. Take your sleeping bag and camp out in the caverns.

[For the full lowdown on Alabama, contact: Alabama Bureau of Tourism and Travel, 532 South Perry Street, Montgomery, 36104; 800/ALABAMA.]

ALABAMA CLOSE-UP: *Wintzell's Oyster House*

You can get it fancier, but you won't get it any fresher or more honest-to-goodness than the Gulf Coast seafood served at Wintzell's Oyster House in Mobile. Chances are you won't find anybody else's surroundings nearly as entertaining, either, because every available square inch of the bustling place is covered with the sardonic wit and wisdom ("When a Little Shot Gets Half Shot—He Thinks He Is a Big Shot") of its late founder, J. Oliver Wintzell. Every oyster lover worth his Tabasco knows about Wintzell's ("Oysters fried, stewed, and nude"), and so does most everybody else who is partial to good Gulf Coast seafood. The wisecracks and the fair prices make it all the more worth your while.

Where to Go for a Good Time in

ARKANSAS

Annual Events

JANUARY
Bald Eagle Watches, Heber Springs, Mount Ida.
Civil War Re-enactment, Gillett.

FEBRUARY
Wild Turkey Calling Contest, Marshall.

MARCH
World Walleye Classic, Fairfield Bay.
Mid-South Gospel Quartet Convention, Jonesboro.
Fiddlers Jamboree, Harrison.

APRIL
Barbershoppers In Concert, Eureka Springs.
Ozark Folk Festival and Craft Guild Show, Mountain View.
Charity Horse Show, Batesville.

MAY
Toad Suck Daze, Conway.
Armadillo Festival, Hamburg.
Antiques Show and Heritage Crafts Fair, War Eagle.
Old Fort Days Rodeo, Fort Smith.

JUNE
Diamond Festival, Murfreesboro.
Lum and Abner Days, Mena.
Western Film and Music Festival, Mountain View.
Bluegrass Association Festival, Otto.

JULY
Rodeo of the Ozarks, Springdale.
Independence Day Horseshoe Tournament, Lake Chicot State Park.
Battle Re-enactment, Bull Shoals, Helena.

AUGUST
Turtle Derby, Gould.
Grape Festival, Tontitown.
Sundown to Sunup Gospel Sing, Springdale.
Old Soldiers Reunion, Heber Springs.

SEPTEMBER
Jazz Festival, Eureka Springs.
Grand Prairie Festival of the Arts, Stuttgart.

OCTOBER
National Wild Turkey Calling Contest and Turkey Trot Festival, Yellville.
Apple Festival, Lincoln.
Frontier Days, Washington.
State Fair and Livestock Show, Little Rock.

NOVEMBER
National Bluegrass Fiddlers Championship, Mountain View.
World's Championship Duck-Calling Contest and Wings over the Prairie Festival, Stuttgart.
Ozark Folk Fest, Eureka Springs.

DECEMBER
Home Tours, Little Rock, Eureka Springs, Helena, Rogers.
Re-enactment of the Battle of Prairie Grove, Prairie Grove Battlefield State Park.

NOT TO BE MISSED

An eclectic selection of Arkansas attractions

• **See history and prosperity preserved** in Little Rock's Quapaw Quarter, the original city site and heart of its antebellum and Victorian heritage. Don't miss the prized Arkansas Territorial Restoration (fourteen significant structures) or the Old State House (Doric architecture at its grandest).

• **Visit Eureka Springs,** Bethlehem of Bible Belt folklore. See the seven-story-tall Christ of the Ozarks statue and a dramatic performance of the great Passion Play. Tour the Christ Only Art Gallery, the Bible Museum, Inspirational Wood Carving Gallery, and the fifty-acre new Holy Land to complete your uplifting outing.

• **Hike the mountainside trails** of White Rock Mountain in the Ozark National Forest for spectacular bluff vantages and secluded wilderness settings. Extend your trek on the neighboring Ozark Highlands Trail.

• **Go West** with a trip to Fort Smith and nearby Van Buren, pioneer outposts and stopping-off points to and from the western frontier. See where the Wild West, the Old South, and Indian cultures converged and the landmarks and legacies are preserved in their honor. In Fort Smith, tour Fort Smith National Historic Site (where Hanging Judge Isaac C. Parker restored law and order), the Old Fort Museum, and Belle Grove Historic District; in Van Buren don't miss Historic Old Main Street (a handsome ten-block area), the Frisco Depot, and the Fairview Cemetery.

• **Round up the family** and saddle up for a dude ranch vacation in the Ozarks.

• **Get a taste of Arkansas's century-old wine heritage** in Wiederkehr Village near Clarksville, where you can tour and sample the fruits of its four wineries.

• **Challenge the state records for rainbow trout** with a float trip down the famed White River, trout fishermen's paradise, starting near Bull Shoals Lake. Head south to Heber Springs and the Little Red River for more prime lunker casting.

• **Pay a visit to the homeplace of Ozark homespun,** the Ozark Folk Center near Mountain View. Browse the authentic crafts and skills of Arkansas' mountain culture; enjoy spirited performances of music, dance, and narratives of Ozark history.

• **Dig for diamonds and semi-precious stones** at the Crater of Diamonds State Park near Murfreesboro. Once you're in the park you can keep all you find, and quite a few keepers (more than 65,000) have been unearthed there.

● **Canoe between soaring lime-stone bluffs** overlooking the Buffalo National River. Tackle its white water sections or leisurely float on calmer stretches; over 125 miles to choose from.

● **Don your waders** and set your sights on the finest duck hunting anywhere, with a November visit to the Mississippi flyway around Stuttgart.

Do it in style with a helping hand from one of several area hunting clubs whose acreage lies beneath the prime skies of migrating quarry and whose hospitality is southern all the way.

[To get the full lowdown on Arkansas, contact: Arkansas Department of Parks and Tourism, One Capitol Mall, Little Rock, 72201; 800/NATURAL.]

ARKANSAS CLOSE-UP: *Hot Springs National Park*

Even before statehood, Arkansas was known far and wide for the thermal waters that gushed from natural springs in its Ouachita Mountains. By the early 1800s, Hot Springs had become akin to a nineteenth-century Golden Door spa; its elegant bathhouses and hotels were patronized by the wealthy and famous. Like these well-heeled visitors, the Indians, and even Hernando De Soto before them, folks today flock to Hot Springs National Park to relish the beneficial (and, some swear, medicinal) proper-

ties of the ever-flowing springs, warmed deep underground by near-molten rock. Like almost all popular tourist attractions, Hot Springs is not exempt from campy commercialism (an alligator farm and wax museum beckon, for instance), but the park itself continues to fascinate and refresh its guests. So take a tour of yesteryear's ornate structures on Bathhouse Row and then partake of the relaxing warm waters in the park's special facilities.

Bathhouse Row at Hot Springs National Park

Where to Go for a Good Time in

GEORGIA

Annual Events

JANUARY
Rattlesnake Roundup, Whigham.
Martin Luther King Week, Atlanta.

FEBRUARY
Georgia Heritage Celebration, Savannah.
Quail Unlimited Celebrity Hunt, Albany.

MARCH
Georgia Cherry Blossom Festival, Macon.
St. Patrick's Day Celebration and Parade, Savannah.
Harness Horse Festival, Hawkinsville.
Rattlesnake Roundup, Claxton.

APRIL
Mayhaw Festival, Colquitt.
Atlanta Steeplechase, Cumming.
Masters Golf Tournament, Augusta.
Rose Festival, Thomasville.

MAY
Cotton Pickin' Country Fair, Gay.
Chehaw National Indian Festival, Albany.
Scottish Highland Games, Savannah.
Masters Water Ski Tournament, Callaway Gardens.
Storytelling Festival, Atlanta.

JUNE
Hot-Air Balloon Festival, Helen.
Gold-panning Championships, Dahlonega.

JULY
Peachtree Road Race, Atlanta.
Shakespeare Festival, Atlanta.
Steam Engine Festival, Cumming.

AUGUST
Georgia Mountain Fair and Country Music Festival, Hiawassee.
Gospel Sing, Waycross.
Beach Music Festival, Jekyll Island.

SEPTEMBER
Clogging Hoedown, Tifton.
Mountain Music and Crafts Festival, Dahlonega.
Open Bass Tournament/Rodeo, Eatonton.
Arts Festival, Atlanta.

OCTOBER
Fair of 1850, Lumpkin.
Brown's Crossing Craftsmen Fair, Milledgeville.
Sorghum Festival, Blairsville.
Blue Ridge Divide Arts & Crafts Festival, Mountain City.
Southern Open PGA Tournament, Pine Mountain.

NOVEMBER
Cane Grindings and Syrup Making, Oatland Island.
Swine Time Festival, Climax.

DECEMBER
Home Tours, Macon, Dalton, Savannah, St. Simons Island, Marietta, Eatonton.
Christmas Open Lighthouse, Tybee Island.
Christmas at Callanwolde, Atlanta.

NOT TO BE MISSED

An eclectic selection of Georgia attractions

• **Pay a visit to Atlanta's Varsity,** world's largest drive-in (and eat-in) and renowned mecca for all lovers of "dogs." Nothing else like it anywhere.

• **Take off for a winter quail-hunting weekend** to the legendary "Golden Triangle" of the Georgia plains. Experienced or wet-behind-the-ears welcome.

• **Make an Uncle Remus pilgrimage** in homage to the beloved Br'er Rabbit tales. Visit the Wren's Nest, Atlanta home of author Joel Chandler Harris; while there, bend your ear toward a resident storyteller for an Uncle Remus tale. Then head to Eatonton, Harris's hometown, to see the commemorative Uncle Remus Museum in a log cabin and the Br'er Rabbit statue.

• **Explore the mysterious Okefenokee Swamp** with a guided wilderness canoe trip and a visit to the Heritage Center near Waycross.

• **Visit Rabun Gap,** where the Foxfire tradition was started, and neighboring Dillard and Clayton for an afternoon of things Appalachian.

• **See where the fate of the Confederate army was sealed** at Chickamauga and Chattanooga National Battlefield Park, Fort Oglethorpe. Review the events of the decisive 1863 battles and examine an extensive array of weaponry.

• **Witness the delivery and adoption of those huggable Cabbage Patch Kids** at Babyland General Hospital in Cleveland.

• **Follow the antebellum trail** for a weekend sojourn through the towns and homes of the genteel Old South: Athens, Madison, Eatonton, Milledgeville, Clinton, and Macon.

• **Ferry over to Cumberland Island National Seashore,** an undisturbed preserve of seaside flora and fauna. Take your backpack and sleep under the stars. Only 300 people are allowed to visit daily.

• **Pay tribute to a King and a president in one mind-boggling day.** Begin with a tour of the Martin Luther King, Jr., National Historical Site in Atlanta, where you'll find his birth home, his pulpit at Ebenezer Baptist Church, and the Center for Nonviolent Social Change. A short drive away, you'll find the Carter Presidential Center, memorial to Jimmy Carter's days in the White House and meeting place for foreign affairs scholars.

• **Spend a weekend in Savannah,** a charming and proud seaport city and Georgia's first settlement. Stroll the historic district, laced with its original twenty-one "squares" of half-acre parks, more than 1,100 restored buildings, and charming broad avenues lined with live oaks. Tour the waterfront district, rejuvenated center of commerce and shipping (and now shopping). Visit its historic homes and churches and the Ships of the Sea museum; venture to Skidaway Island's marine science complex. Explore some of the state's oldest standing forts, Jackson and Pulaski.

• **Come summer, pick your own peaches** in orchards around Perry—fresh, juicy, and cheap.

• **Visit a former stronghold of the rich and famous, Jekyll Island,** where Rockefellers, Goodyears, Goulds, and so forth, once spent indolent vacations removed from the hoi polloi. Then head to the current stomping grounds of well-bred and well-heeled families from the Northeast to the South, Sea Island (take lots of pink and green to wear).

• **Hike the trail up Rabun Bald Mountain** to its 4,660-foot elevation. Soak in the panoramic view of the Chattahoochee National Forest.

• **Experience firsthand the formidable white waters of the Chatooga River** (where the film *Deliverance* was made) with an adventurous raft or canoe trip.

[For the full lowdown on Georgia, contact: Georgia Department of Industry and Trade, Post Office Box 1776, Atlanta, 30301; 404/656-3590.]

GEORGIA CLOSE-UP: *Rebel-rousing Stone Mountain Park*

You might care to go to Stone Mountain Park (outside of Atlanta) for the family recreation this 3,200-acre park and resort offers, and probably to admire its astonishing 825-foot-high mass of exposed granite. As a Southerner, there is another reason you *have* to go. At Stone Mountain you'll encounter two of the most unabashed tributes to the motherland around and, with them, a glimpse into the southern experience: (1) the Confederate Memorial Carving, a massive and inspiring tribute to the Lost Cause on one side of the mountain, featuring Generals Robert E. Lee and "Stonewall" Jackson, and Confederate President Jefferson Davis on horseback; (2) the Laser Show, a yee-haw, yahoo crowd-pleasing summertime laser phantasmagoria on the mountain's north face, which concludes with an always rebel-rousing finale of "Dixie" and fireworks.

Where to Go for a Good Time in

KENTUCKY

Annual Events

JANUARY
Kentucky Craft Market, Louisville.

FEBRUARY
Championship Tractor Pull, Louisville.

MARCH
Storytelling Weekend, Greenup County.
Humana Festival of New American Plays, Louisville.

APRIL
Hillbilly Days, Pikeville.
American Quilter's Society National Show, Paducah.
Kentucky Derby Festival, Louisville.

MAY
Highland Games and Gathering of Scottish Clans, Glasgow.
Mountain Laurel Festival, Pineville.
Shaped Note Singing Convention, Benton.
Kentucky Derby, Louisville.
Long Rifle Frolics, Butler County and Land Between the Lakes.

JUNE
Shaker Festival, South Union.
National Mountain-Style Square Dance and Clogging Festival, Slade.
Festival of the Bluegrass, Lexington.
The Egyptian Event (Egyptian-Arabian Horse Show), Lexington.
W. C. Handy Blues and Barbeque Festival, Henderson.
Appalachian Celebration, Morehead.

JULY
State Championship Old Time Fiddlers' Contest, Rough River Dam State Park.

International Ventriloquists Convention, Fort Mitchell/Kenton County.
Junior League Horse Show, Lexington.

AUGUST
Pioneer Days Festival, Harrodsburg.
Battle of Richmond Living History Weekend, Madison County.
State Fair, Louisville.

SEPTEMBER
Cow Days, Greensburg.
Highlands Folk Festival, Wiley State Park.
Corn Island Storytelling Festival, Louisville.
Rolley-Hole Marble Tournament, Tompkinsville.
Daniel Boone Pioneer Festival, Winchester.

OCTOBER
Tobacco Festivals, Russellville, Bloomfield, Hart County.
Red Crow Indian Council Pow Wow, Clermont.
Civil War Re-enactments, Butler County Park, Belmont State Park, London, Perryville.
Appalachian Folk Music Festival, Berea College, Berea.

NOVEMBER
International Livestock Exposition, Louisville.
Book Fair, Frankfort.

DECEMBER
Home Tours, Louisville, Bardstown, Frankfort, Bowling Green, Harrodsburg.
Frontier Christmas, Washington.

NOT TO BE MISSED

An eclectic selection of Kentucky attractions

• **Have yourself a horsey time** in Lexington and Louisville, twin hubs of the Bluegrass region. In Lexington head first to Kentucky Horse Park for an all-day tribute to horse history, breeding, raising, riding, and racing. Pay a visit to the Horse Center, Keeneland Race Course, Red Mile Harness Track, and, of course, world-famous Spendthrift Farm before you leave. In Louisville make tracks to Churchill Downs and the onsite Kentucky Derby Museum, then wrap up your equine explorations with a wager at the Louisville Downs harness races.

• **Spend a back-country weekend of hiking and camping** amidst the pristine rivers, gorges, and wilderness of Big South Fork National Recreation Area.

• **Angle your way to the annual April crappie runs** at Kentucky Lake for some of the best biting you've seen in a long time.

• **Step into Appalachian culture in Berea.** See the workings of Southern Highlands life and lore at the Appalachian Museum, admire the traditional handiwork of Berea College crafts, then observe the art of handweaving in the loomhouse of Churchill Weavers.

• **Recount America's Boy Scout history** at the National Museum of the Boy Scouts, which includes fifty-three original Norman Rockwell paintings of Boy Scout life in its installations.

• **Put Kentucky into historical perspective** with a visit to Frankfort. Trace state history at the Kentucky History Museum, Military History Museum, and the Frankfort Cemetery, burial grounds of famous pioneers and politicians. See striking examples of architecture: Beaux Arts (Governor's Mansion), Federal (Vest-Lindsey House), Greek Revival (Ward Hall), and Georgian (Liberty Hall). Check out the early farm implements at Luscher's Museum of the American Farmer.

• **Watch the step-by-step production of the Corvette** in Bowling Green at the world's only Chevrolet Corvette facility.

• **View more than 125 original pieces from John James Audubon's remarkable "Birds of America"** series at the museum in his namesake state park.

• **Enter the Shaker era** at the Shaker Village of Pleasant Hill near Harrodsburg, where thirty original buildings of this 1805 community are preserved on 2,700 acres of picturesque countryside. Admire their distinctive architecture, furniture, and tools, observe demonstrations of the society's life, and walk the peaceful grounds. Stay a while. You can dine and sleep there, too.

• **Descend into the world's largest cave system** at the amazing Mammoth Cave National Park, with over 300 miles of mapped passageways. Take a sweater; this is one place the sun never shines.

• **Relive the history and charm of the once-flourishing nineteenth-century town,** Bardstown. Tour a living-history village, mansions, museums including the fascinating Mini-ature Soldier Museum, and visit the Old Talbott Tavern, America's oldest stagecoach stop.

• **Discover prehistoric Indian culture** from A.D. 800 to 1350. Burial sites, home sites, temple mounds, and artifacts at Wickliffe Mounds, Wickliffe.

[To get the full lowdown on Kentucky, contact: Kentucky Department of Travel Development, Capital Plaza Tower, Frankfort, 40601; 800/225-TRIP.]

KENTUCKY CLOSE-UP: *Vice Tour*

Kentucky is home state to numerous distilleries and cigarette factories. So why not take a few side trips to see what they're all about? These folks are more than happy to have you pay them a visit. Begin your touring in Louisville at the Phillip Morris USA tobacco-processing and cigarette-packing facility. Proceed to Frankfort, home to Ancient Age, Old Grand-Dad, and Old Crow distilleries. Resume your vice tour in Bardstown, home of Getz Museum of Whiskey History, and Jim Beam, Heaven Hill, and Evan Williams whiskies. Should you crave even more, you can find it in Loretto (Maker's Mark), Owensboro (Glenmore), and Lawrenceville (Wild Turkey).

Maker's Mark Distillery, Loretto

Where to Go for a Good Time in

LOUISIANA

Annual Events

JANUARY
Sugar Bowl Football Classic, New Orleans.
Fur and Wildlife Festival, Cameron.

FEBRUARY
Mardi Gras (some years in March), New Orleans, Lafayette, et al.
Civil War Encampment, Merryville.
LSU Championship Rodeo, Baton Rouge.

MARCH
Audubon Pilgrimage, St. Francisville.
Cajun Fun Fest, New Iberia.

APRIL
PGA Golf Classic, New Orleans.
French Acadian Music Festival, Abbeville.
Creole Festival, Houma.
Cajun Joke Telling Festival, Opelousas.
Jazz and Heritage Festival, New Orleans.
Louisiana State Fiddlers Championship, Marthaville.

MAY
Crawfish Festival (even-numbered years), Breaux Bridge.
Mayhaw Festival, Marion.

JUNE
Pirogue Races, Slidell.
Bayou Lacombe Crab Festival, Lacombe.
Possum Festival, Arcadia.
Jambalaya Festival, Sorrento.

JULY
Northwestern Folk Festival, Natchitoches.

Cajun Bastille Day, Baton Rouge.
International Tarpon Rodeo, Grand Isle.
Accordian Festival, Breaux Bridge.

AUGUST
South Lafourche Seafood Festival, Galliano.
Shrimp Festival, Delcambre.
Southwest Louisiana Zydeco Music Festival, Plaisance.

SEPTEMBER
Festival du Lapin, Grand Prairie.
Frog Festival, Rayne.
Sugar Cane Festival and Fair, New Iberia.
Shrimp and Petroleum Festival, Morgan City.
Square Dance Festival, Lake Charles.

OCTOBER
International Rice Festival, Crowley.
State Fair, Shreveport.
Sauce Piquante Festival, Raceland.
International Acadian Festival, Plaquemine.
Prison Rodeo, Angola.

NOVEMBER
Pecan Festival, Colfax.
Plantation Fall Festival, Destrehan.
Christmas Boat Parade, New Roads.

DECEMBER
Festival de Grand Coteau, Grand Coteau.
Home Tours, Alexandria, Houma, Baton Rouge, New Iberia.
A Cajun Christmas, Lafayette.
Festival of the Bonfires, Gramercy to Lutcher.

NOT TO BE MISSED

An eclectic selection of Louisiana attractions

● **Get duded up for an evening of country/western two-stepping** at the ever-popular "Louisiana Hayride," live radio broadcast and dance every Saturday night in Shreveport. More music-hall dancing (same time) at the Old South Jamboree near Walker.

● **Cook up a Creole meal** in short order with a three-hour hands-on class at the New Orleans School of Cooking.

● **Go fish, offshore style,** in the coastal waters of the Gulf of Mexico for such gamefish as mackerel, marlin, pompano, snapper, and tarpon. Grand Isle is a favorite charter boat point.

● **Tour the magnificent treasures of Louisiana's plantation country** with a drive on River Road (between New Orleans and Baton Rouge) or around the town of St. Francisville. See for yourself how good the good life could be if you were a wealthy planter before the War and even experience it in those mansions with bed and breakfast accommodations.

● **See Mardi Gras in the making** at Mardi Gras World in New Orleans, where the floats and ornaments of the annual carnival are constructed. Contrast Mardi Gras present with those past by visiting the Presbytere and Old U.S. Mint, which house Mardi Gras exhibits and memorabilia in their collections.

● **Watch the making of a tastemaker** on Avery Island, home of the famous Tabasco Sauce, with a tour of the century-old process. Then explore the 200-acre Jungle Gardens and Bird Sanctuary, exotic living legacy of Tabasco's founding family.

● **Venture into the mystical and mysterious** at the Voodoo Museum in New Orleans's French Quarter. Take the museum-guided voodoo walking tour, then visit the grave of Marie Laveau, legendary voodoo queen of the city, at the St. Louis No. 1. Cemetery.

● **Make a fall excursion to Louisiana's oldest town,** Natchitoches,

Jackson Square, New Orleans

during its open house tour. Sample the charm bestowed by 250 years of prosperous and gracious living with a distinguished French heritage.

• **Stroll the colonnaded galleries and shops of the famed Old French Market** in New Orleans. Savor every tourist's just reward: steaming hot *café au lait* and those incomparable beignets at Café du Monde.

• **Get face-to-face with the alligators** of Bayou Country on a wetlands boat tour. Cruise through the cypress swamplands and marshes for a close-up look at nutria, raccoon, egrets, herons, alligators, and more in their wilderness habitat.

• **Explore Acadiana, heartland of French Louisiana,** where French Acadians and expatriates of the French Revolution once settled. Trace the tragedy of Evangeline (immortalized in Longfellow's poem) and her fellow Acadians with visits to the old Evangeline Oak in St. Martinville, her grave at St. Martin de Tours Catholic Church, and the close-by commemorative area, featuring an eighteenth-century Acadian plantation house and period artifacts.

• **Place your bets on Thoroughbred racehorses,** spring till fall, at racetracks in Lafayette, Vinton, Bossier City, New Orleans, and Kenner.

[For the full lowdown on Louisiana, contact: Louisiana Office of Tourism, Post Office Box 94291, Baton Rouge, 70804; 800/33 GUMBO.]

LOUISIANA CLOSE-UP: *New Orleans' St. Charles Line Streetcar*

Ride the tracks of New Orleans history (exact change only, please) on the 150-year-old St. Charles Line streetcar, one of the South's beloved antiques of transit. The sole survivor of a trolley system that once laced the city, the St. Charles line still carries over 20,000 riders daily. You haven't lived until you've ridden the streetcar, so make the best of your outing when you do. Board downtown at Canal and Carondelet streets and settle into a windowside wooden bench for the one-and-one-half-hour circuit. The St. Charles will carry you through the heart of the venerable Garden District, where the gracious architecture of antebellum New Orleans is in plentiful supply; past the campuses of Tulane and Loyola universities, and finally to the end of the line, where there's further fascination for those who choose to disembark: the Audubon Zoo.

Where to Go for a Good Time in

MISSISSIPPI

Annual Events

FEBRUARY
Dixie National Livestock Show and Rodeo, Jackson.
Krewe of Phoenix Mardi Gras, Natchez.

MARCH
Spring Pilgrimages, see chapter 2.

APRIL
Natchez Trace Festival, Kosciusko.
Crawfish Festival, Biloxi.
Dulcimer Day, Tishomingo State Park.
Confederate Heritage Month, Vicksburg.

MAY
Jimmie Rodgers Memorial Festival, Meridian.
Shrimp Festivals and Blessings of Fleets, Biloxi, Pass Christian, Pascagoula.
Grand Prix Catfish Races, Greenville.

JUNE
B. B. King Festival, Indianola.
International Ballet Competition (1994, 1998), Jackson.
Magnolia State Bluegrass Festival, Wiggins.

JULY
Choctaw Indian Fair, Philadelphia.
Deep-Sea Fishing Rodeo, Gulfport.

Rhythm and Blues Festival, Chunky.
Civil War Re-enactment, Vicksburg.

AUGUST
Kudzu in Yazoo Hawg Day, Yazoo City.
William Faulkner Conference, Oxford.
Cotton Row on Parade, Greenwood.
Neshoba County Fair, Philadelphia.

SEPTEMBER
Delta Blues Festival, Greenville.
Seafood Festival, Biloxi.
Muscadine Jubilee, Pelahatchie.

OCTOBER
Antique Tractor and Engine Show, Sardis.
International Red Beans and Rice Festival, Jackson.
Mullet Festival, Gautier.
State Fair, Jackson.
Tennessee Williams Festival, Jackson.

NOVEMBER
Mistletoe Market Place, Jackson.
Wild Game Cookoff Championship, Biloxi.

DECEMBER
Home Tours, Natchez, Meridian, Greenwood, Columbus, Hattiesburg.

NOT TO BE MISSED

An eclectic selection of Mississippi attractions

• **See the humble birthplace of a King** with a trip to Tupelo, where you'll find the two-room shotgun house in which Elvis Presley was born. See also the next-door Memorial Chapel, legacy of love from the King's loyal followers.

• **Admire the graceful artistry of the highly sought pottery of acclaimed George Ohr and Walter Anderson.** In Biloxi, Ohr's handiwork can be found at Art By Moran's and the Mississippi Museum of Art, Gulf Coast. In Ocean Springs, Anderson's wares are on display at Shearwater Pottery. Known also for his striking murals, Anderson's brushwork is showcased at the Ocean Springs Community Center and the nearby Walter Anderson Cottage.

• **Step back into time**—36 million years, that is—with an exploration of the Mississippi Petrified Forest near Flora. The only one of its kind in the eastern United States.

• **Make tracks to the heartland of the blues.** Things take a historical perspective at the Delta Blues Museum in Clarksdale's Carnegie Public Library, a repository of blues artifacts, memorabilia, and arcana. Close by is the Stackhouse Delta Record Mart and Rooster Blues Records, treasure trove of obscure and vintage blues recordings. Over in Oxford, the University of

Mississippi Blues Archive boasts a substantial library of recordings, exhibits and the personal collection of B. B. King himself.

• **Savor the southern wines** of the muscadine and scuppernong vines with excursions to Almarla Vineyards (Matherville) and Old South Winery (Natchez).

• **Travel by boat to explore the islands of the Gulf Coast National Seashore** in the Mississippi Sound. Visit Fort Massachusetts, on Ship Island, built by the Confederacy but seized by Union forces and used to imprison Confederate soldiers. Discover the coastal habitats of Horn and Petit Bois islands, both wildlife sanctuaries and nesting places for wintering birds (wilderness lovers can set up camp on Horn Island).

D'Evereux Mansion, Natchez

• **Make a spring pilgrimage** to the magnificent homes of the wealthy Old South in the state that invented the annual rite (see chapter 4).

• **Enter the animal world** at the Jackson Zoological Park, just-like-home habitat to living creatures from all parts of the planet. Then see suspended animation—of a different sort—at the Museum of Natural Science, repository of mounted wildlife specimens, aquaria, and ecological depictions.

• **Visit the antebellum home of a literary giant** and favorite native son in Oxford at Rowan Oak, the secluded residence where William Faulkner penned his prizewinning works.

• **Paddle a canoe down the Chunky River** south of Meridian for a backwaters pleasure trip (favorite scenic spot: the tiered, fifty-foot-tall Dunn's Falls). Or put in on the banks of Bull Mountain Creek upstate and cast off in search of spotted bass and catfish.

• **Look away to the land of cotton** with a visit to the Delta town of Greenwood during the fall harvest. See the bustling Cotton Row at the height of trading activity, then observe the glory days of cotton re-enacted at Florewood River Plantation (you can even pick your own cotton).

• **Travel by bicycle** over the stomping grounds of Indians, DeSoto, and frontier explorers on the ancient and scenic Natchez Trace Parkway. Narrate your overland tour by reading the markers of historic and natural interest.

• **Seek out the memorabilia of Mississippi legends** with trips to the Casey Jones Museum in Vaughan and the Jimmie Rodgers Museum in Meridian.

[For the full lowdown on Mississippi, contact: Mississippi Department of Economic Development, Division of Tourism, Post Office Box 849, Jackson, 39205; 800/647-2290.]

MISSISSIPPI CLOSE-UP: *Vicksburg National Battlefield Park*

For forty-seven days it was the sight of one of the War's fiercest sieges, but the bounty was worth all possible sacrifice to both sides: control of the mighty Mississippi, lifeline of the Confederate States of America. Beyond the river bluffs spread the 1,800 acres of Vicksburg National Military Park, site of the bitter, protracted struggle. Traversing this territory (rent an audio cassette from the Park Service) will put the siege in very human terms, the tragic story unfolding over the battleground of re-created forts, trenches, and artillery installations. More than 1,400 markers, memorials, and monuments (plus the Vicksburg National Cemetery) describe the grim events of spring 1863, when more than 17,000 soldiers of the Blue and Gray fought to the death.

211

Where to Go for a Good Time in

NORTH CAROLINA

Annual Events

FEBRUARY
Camellia Show, Charlotte.
Goodwrench 500 NASCAR Race, Rockingham.
Gospel Celebration, Charlotte.

MARCH
Old Time Fiddlers and Blue Grass Convention, Mooresville.
Hounds Hunter Trials, Southern Pines.

APRIL
Azalea Festival, Wilmington.
PGA Open, Greensboro.
National Whistlers Convention, Louisburg.
Steeplechase Races, Tryon, Southern Pines.
Dogwood Festival, Statesville.

MAY
Tarheel Storytelling Festival, Winston-Salem.
Gee Haw Whimmy Diddle World Competition, Asheville.
Wooden Boat Show, Beaufort.
Sheep Dog Trial, Pittsboro.
Champion Spark Plug 300 NASCAR Grand National and Coca-Cola 600 NASCAR Winston Cup Races, Concord.

JUNE
Annual Storytelling Festival, Beech Mountain.
Annual Singing on the Mountain, Linville.
Seafood Festival and Blessing of the Fleet, Wanchese.
Rhododendron Festival, Bakersville.

JULY
Shindig on the Green, Asheville.
Brevard Festival of the Arts, Brevard.
Folkmoot USA, Waynesville.

AUGUST
Shrimp Festival, Sneads Ferry.
Virginia Dare Gossyp Festival, Manteo.

SEPTEMBER
Bald Is Beautiful Convention, Morehead City.
State Chili Championship, Clemmons.
Turkey Festival, Raeford.
State Championship Horse Show, Raleigh.
Currituck Wildlife Festival, Barco.

OCTOBER
Scottish Festival and Highland Games, Red Springs and Singleton Meadows.
BBQ Festival, Lexington.
Any and All Dog Show, Tryon.
Oyster Festival, Shallotte.
State Fair, Raleigh.

NOVEMBER
Mid-Atlantic Championship Rodeo, Raleigh.
Carolina Craftsmen's Christmas Classic Exhibition, Greensboro.
Festival of Trees, Wilmington.

DECEMBER
Home Tours, Hillsborough, Wilmington, Waynesville, Burlington, Fayetteville, Tarboro, Winston-Salem.
Christmas Guild Fair of Southern Highland Handicraft Guild, Asheville.

NOT TO BE MISSED

An eclectic selection of North Carolina attractions

- **Strike out on a wildflower trek** in Blue Ridge Mountains, lofty stage for ever-changing carpets of color, including flaming azaleas and dogwood (spring), mountain laurel (May), and the glorious rhododendron (June).

- **Venture on a vice tour** around the state, home to several cigarette manufacturers (R. J. Reynolds Tobacco, Winston-Salem; Phillip Morris, Concord; American Tobacco, Reidsville) and brewery (Stroh Brewery, Winston-Salem).

- **Take a waterfall tour** (and take a picnic, too) in Nantahala National Forest along U.S. Highway 64. Enjoy the captivating beauty of such cascades as Bird Rock, Toxaway, Whitewater (441 feet), Rainbow, and Bridal Veil Falls. Conclude your tour with sojourns to nearby Dry Falls and Cullasaja.

- **Savor the gingerbread charm of Historic Oakwood** neighborhood in Raleigh, tree-lined treasury with more than four hundred elegant examples of Victorian architecture.

- **Soar amidst the mountains and amongst the champions.** Go hang gliding at Grandfather Mountain near Linville.

- **Review your Revolutionary War history** with a stop at Moores Creek National Battlefield near Wilmington, site of a decisive battle that helped ensure colonists' freedom from Britain.

- **Scuba a shipwreck** (choose from more than 400), macabre underwater reminders of the treacherous North Carolina coast.

- **Learn the ways of the Cherokee Indians** at Qualla Boundary Reserve with a trip to Museum of the Cherokee Indian, Oconaluftee Indian Village, and Qualla Arts and Crafts Mutual. Contrast their proud heritage with Cherokee's Santa's Land Fantasy Park.

- **Expand your historical horizons** with an excursion to Old Salem. This Moravian congregational town founded in 1766 features more than sixty rebuilt/restored structures. Then dig deeper into the past at Historic Bethabara Park, location of the Moravians' first North Carolina settlement and now site of modern Winston-Salem.

- **Learn the lessons of coastal existence** for man and nature at the North Carolina Maritime Hampton Museum in Beaufort. Sign up for a day's guided field trip of birding, fossil hunting, flatland and marsh exploration, shelling, or wildflowers.

- **Ski the South's favorite winter slopes** at Beech and Sugar mountains, Cataloochee, and Wolf Laurel.

• **Collect one-of-a-kind examples of mountainmade handiwork** with an excursion to the Southern Highland Handicraft Guild's Folk Art Center, east of Asheville, a respected source for the pottery, needlework, crafts, and handcarved items (like whimmy diddles) of the mountainfolk culture.

• **Discover the historic Atlantic coast settlements** of the New World around the Outer Banks: Edenton, a 265-year-old colonial coast village brimming with historical sites and architectural treasures; New Bern, a former colonial capital and home to the distinguished Tryon Palace; and Beaufort, charming seacoast town.

[For the full lowdown on North Carolina, contact: North Carolina Travel and Tourism Division, Department of Commerce, 430 North Salisbury Street, Raleigh, 27611; 800/VISITNC.]

NORTH CAROLINA CLOSE-UP: *Biltmore House and Gardens*

You'd swear you were in the Loire Valley of France upon sighting the majestic chateau, but you're near Asheville, overlooking the Swannanoa and French Broad valleys at a superlative vantage point: Biltmore House. This is the house that money built—lots of it—to fulfill a dream of Cornelius Vanderbilt's erudite grandson, George. Completed in 1895, the fantasyland mansion, its grand furnishings, and expansive gardens (designed by Frederick Law Olmstead) are all remarkable statements of beauty, design, and ingenuity. You can see the splendor of Biltmore House and Gardens (and its new winery) for yourself; more than 50 of its 200-plus rooms are open for exploration if you're willing to spring the price of admission (not cheap, but then again, neither was the house).

The Biltmore House

Where to Go for a Good Time in

SOUTH CAROLINA

Annual Events

JANUARY

Grand American Coon Hunt, Orangeburg.

Polo Matches (through April), Aiken.

FEBRUARY

Southeastern Wildlife Exposition, Charleston.

Lowcountry Oyster Festival, Charleston.

MARCH

Annual Triple Crown (Harness Race, Thoroughbred Trials and Steeplechase), Aiken.

Governor's Frog Jump and Egg Striking Contest (Easter Weekend), Springfield.

Carolina Cup Races, Camden.

Home and Plantation Tours, Beaufort, Charleston, Conway, Georgetown.

APRIL

Stone Soup Storytelling Festival, Woodruff.

Festival of Roses, Orangeburg.

Heritage Golf Classic, Hilton Head.

MAY

Spoleto Festival USA, Charleston.

Blue Crab Festival, Little River.

Gullah Festival, Beaufort.

Lowcountry Shrimp Festival and Blessing of Fleet, McClellanville.

JUNE

Watermelon Festival, Hampton.

State Festival of Flowers, Greenwood.

JULY

State Tobacco Festival, Lake City.

Hillbilly Day, Mountain Rest.

Great Waccamaw Riverfest and Raft Race, Conway.

State Peach Festival, Gaffney.

AUGUST

SC Peanut Party, Pelion.

SEPTEMBER

Southern 500 Winston Cup Stock Car Race, Darlington.

Harvest Hoedown Festival, Aynor.

Savannah Valley Heritage Festival, McCormick.

Scottish Games and Highland Gathering, Charleston.

OCTOBER

State Fair, Columbia.

Gopher Hill Festival, Ridgeland.

Pumpkin Festival, Pumpkintown.

State Chili Cook-off, Conway.

Okra Strut, Irmo.

NOVEMBER

Heritage Celebration, St. Helena Island.

Colonial Cup International Steeplechase, Camden.

DECEMBER

Holiday Tours, Abbeville, Camden, Charleston, McConnells, Hilton Head, Pendleton, York.

North-South High School All Star Football Game, Myrtle Beach.

NOT TO BE MISSED

An eclectic selection of South Carolina attractions

• **Go to seed on the perfect plot** with a trip to the George W. Park Seed Company near Greenwood. Gardeners everywhere know their name like the back of their hands. Tour the lush display and test gardens, then take home a fresh supply of *objets d'horticulture.*

• **Make tracks to Thoroughbred territory** around Aiken, where hopes and dreams and lots of money are pinned on horses. No circus horses here, just the highbrow variety, bred and trained for polo (played eight months a year) or to race to the finish at Aiken's annual Triple Crown events (harness and Thoroughbred racing, steeplechasing). A winter colony for America's horsey set during the late nineteenth century, Aiken's historic district bears testament to its past: ninety-room vacation "cottages," unpaved roads and special stop lights for equestrians. Visit during March for the Triple Crown series, memorialized at the Thoroughbred Racing Hall of Fame and maybe settle in the saddle yourself for a ride over the bridle paths of Hitchcock Woods nature preserve.

• **Get a bird's-eye view of St. Helena Sound** from the top of Hunting Island's old lighthouse. Your panorama will include the beaches and marshes of the island (now a state park populated with wild game and migratory birds), the archipelago surrounding Beaufort and Atlantic Ocean horizons.

• **Try for some record smashing** of your own at the state's most famous fishing holes, the Santee Cooper lakes (Lakes Moultrie and Marion, near Charleston), home to the world's heftiest landlocked striped bass, channel catfish, and black crappie.

• **Take a slow tour through the capital of fast cars** at the Stock Car Hall of Fame near Darlington. Admire the world's largest collection of race cars, buckle up for a simulated raceway ride in Richard Petty's Dodge, and see the ones that didn't get away; illegal parts found in race-ready cars.

• **Pass into another world in Charleston,** refined old city of distinguished history, architecture, and family trees. Prepare to be totally charmed by old Charleston's plenitude of seventeenth- and eighteenth-century dwellings (particularly the indigenous "single house") and gardens, noble churches and offices, shops and marketplaces. Gracious living is the watchword here, and it's practiced expertly. Don't miss strolling on the famous bayside Battery Park, venturing to surrounding plantations (see "Close-Up"), feasting on sophisticated Low-Country cuisine, or the opportunity to call a historic inn home for a few nights (bring money).

● **Cavort à la Coney Island** on the shores of the Grand Strand, endless seaside playland and amusement mecca. If you like crowds, wax museums, water slides, souvenir shops, carpet golf, and the like, you'll be in hog heaven in this neck of the woods.

● **Gather while ye may the popular handiworks of South Carolina's coastal cultures.** Pawley's Island hammocks and Low-Country sweetgrass baskets, all handwoven in testament to the state's African and West Indian heritages, are in ready supply.

● **Watch pro-baseball hopefuls** sharpen their skills at farm team match-ups with ballpark visits to the Columbia Mets (New York Mets) or the Charleston Rainbows (San Diego Padres).

[For the full lowdown on South Carolina, contact: South Carolina Division of Tourism, Post Office Box 71, Columbia, 29202; 803/734-0122.]

SOUTH CAROLINA CLOSE-UP: *The Low-Country Plantation Gardens*

They're old, they're big, they're splendid, and they're definitely worth the price of admission. They're the landmark plantations of two distinguished Low-Country dynasties: Drayton Hall and its Magnolia Plantation and Gardens and Middleton Place, gardens, mansion, and stableyard. Within four miles of one another on the Ashley River (near Charleston), both are remarkable heirlooms of early Carolina wealth. At Drayton Hall, c. 1738, you'll find what is considered the nation's finest example of Georgia Palladian architecture, *sans* modernization. Nearby, find the estate's magnificent garden, with its famous tree-sized camellias and abundant azalea beds, plus Drayton's plantation house. There's yet more grandeur and elegance at Middleton Place. Tudor-style home to one of America's founding families and site of Old-World, terraced gardens framed by butterfly lakes and lush ornamental plantings.

Where to Go for a Good Time in

TENNESSEE

Annual Events

FEBRUARY

International Indoor Tennis Tournament, Memphis.

National Field Trial Championship, Grand Junction.

MARCH

International Wine Festival, Knoxville.

State Old Time Fiddlers' Festival, Clarksville.

APRIL

Dogwood Arts Festival, Knoxville.

Mule Day, Columbia.

Spring Wildflower Pilgrimage, Gatlinburg.

MAY

Iroquois Steeplechase, Nashville.

Memphis in May Festivals.

Scottish Festival and Games, Gatlinburg.

Storytelling Festival, Franklin.

JUNE

Riverbend Festival and Great Tennessee River Raft Race, Chattanooga.

International Country Music Fan Fair, Nashville.

Dulcimer and Harp Convention, Cosby.

Rhododendron Festival, Roan.

Covered Bridge Festival, Elizabethton.

JULY

Fiddlers' Jamboree and Crafts Festival, Smithville.

Tennessee-Kentucky Threshermen's Show, Adams.

Uncle Dave Macon Days, Murfreesboro.

St. Jude Golf Classic, Memphis.

AUGUST

Tennessee Walking Horse National Celebration, Shelbyville.

International Grand Championship Walking Horse Show, Murfreesboro.

Elvis International Tribute Week, Memphis.

SEPTEMBER

International Banana Festival, South Fulton.

State Fair, Nashville.

Davy Crockett Days, Rutherford.

OCTOBER

National Storytelling Festival, Jonesborough.

Autumn Leaf Special (Steam Train), Chattanooga.

Museum of Appalachia Fall Homecoming, Norris.

NOVEMBER

Mid-South Arts and Crafts Show, Memphis.

Christmas Lights Festival, Gatlinburg.

DECEMBER

Home Tours, Franklin, Jonesborough, Knoxville, Murfreesboro, Nashville.

Liberty Bowl Football Classic, Memphis.

NOT TO BE MISSED

An eclectic selection of Tennessee attractions

• **Ascend to heights of aged grandeur** at the Great Smoky Mountains National Park. Spectacular and beautiful to see and explore, no matter what time of year.

• **Relive the battles of the War Between the States** at Tennessee's National Military parks, including Chickamauga, Chattanooga, Shiloh, Stones River, and Fort Donelson.

• **Tour Jack Daniel Distillery** in Lynchburg or the George Dickel Distillery in Tullahoma and observe the making of Tennessee's famous sour mash whiskey.

• **Head for the thrills.** Go hang gliding at Raccoon Mountain Flight Park; take a white-water rafting trip on the Ocoee, Big South Fork, or Big Pigeon rivers (recommended for the experienced and adventurous).

• **Visit the mecca of every true-blue country music fan** in Nashville. Head straight for Music Row, heart of Nashville's recording industry. Proceed to the Country Music Hall of Fame and Museum, Ryman Auditorium (first home of the Grand Ole Opry). Tour the homes of country music stars. Spend a day (and night) at Opryland USA theme park; enjoy a show at the Grand Ole Opry or the Nashville Network. Venture out to Music Village USA in Hendersonville, where you'll find the House of Cash, Twitty City, and more music-minded attractions—often live performances, too.

• **Mix the quaint with the tacky** in Gatlinburg and nearby Pigeon Forge. Midst the natural glory of the Smokies is plenty of the garish, like wax museums and foreign-made souvenirs. Yet there's also year-round snow skiing, fascinating subterranean caverns, Dolly Parton's Dollywood, and the traditional, widely admired handiwork of mountain craftspeople. Be sure you ride the Gatlinburg Ski Lift for a panoramic view of the Smokies.

• **Cap off your kitsch quotient** with a trip to Lookout Mountain, home of Rock City ("See seven states!"), Fairyland, and Mother Goose Village. Don't miss the breathtaking climb up (or down) Lookout Mountain on the incredibly steep Incline Railway. Wrap up your excursion with a foray to Ruby Falls and Lookout Mountain Caverns.

• **Do a little energy research of your own** at Oak Ridge, where the nation entered the Atomic Age. Visit the American Museum of Science and Energy and take the Oak Ridge Energy Tour.

• **Visit the Tennessee Walking Horse Breeders and Exhibitors**

Association headquarters in Lewisburg, then tour one of the area's walking horse farms.

• **Explore Memphis.** Tour its Victorian Village Historic District, Pink Palace Museum and Planetarium, Botanic Gardens, and Chucalissa Indian Village. Make a summer's day of it at Mud Island, offshore fun-and-folklore tribute to the mighty Mississippi River. Take a riverboat excursion on the *Memphis Queen.* Hang out at Overton Square. Make the pilgrimage of all blues aficionados, Beale Street, where the blues play on. Visit the home of the King, Graceland, and Sun Studios, where careers of blues and rock and roll legends were launched.

• **Immerse yourself in the ways and lore of Tennessee mountain culture** at the Museum of Appalachia in Norris and the Folklife Center of the Smokies, near Cosby.

• **Spend a winter weekend cross-country skiing** in the rarefied air of Roan Mountain State Resort Park.

[To get the full lowdown on Tennessee, contact: Tennessee Department of Tourist Development, Post Office Box 23170, Nashville, 37202; 615/741-2158.]

TENNESSEE CLOSE-UP: *The Peabody Hotel*

According to author Dave Cohn, the Mississippi Delta begins in the lobby of the Peabody Hotel in Memphis and ends on Catfish Row in Vicksburg. At the Peabody "ultimately you will see everybody who is anybody in the Delta." Restored to its glory of old days (and now on the National Register of Historic Places), the elegant Peabody is the place to see and be seen in Memphis. It's also the place to see the "running of the ducks," a daily procession by the hotel's webbed-footed residents to and from the lobby fountain. To the strains of Sousa's "King Cotton March," they waddle to the fountain at 11:00 A.M. (via red carpet) and depart for their roost at 5:00 P.M. with similar fanfare. Naturally, duck motifs abound at the Peabody.

The "running of the ducks"

Where to Go for a Good Time in

VIRGINIA

Annual Events

FEBRUARY
Wildfowl Carving and Art Exhibition, Richmond.
George Washington's Birthday Celebration, Alexandria.

MARCH
Highland County Maple Festival, Monterey.
Crawford Bay Crew Classic, Portsmouth.
Kite Festival, Lorton.

APRIL
Virginia Horse Festival, Lexington.
Historic Garden Week, statewide.
Dogwood Festival, Vinton.

MAY
Coursing Hound Field Trials, Orange County.
Shenandoah Apple Blossom Festival, Winchester.
State Chili Cook-off, Roanoke.
Battle of Fredericksburg Re-enactment, Fredericksburg.

JUNE
Tidewater Scottish Festival and Clan Gathering, Norfolk.
Virginia Wine Festival, The Plains.
Virginia Indian Heritage Festival, Williamsburg.
Roanoke Valley Horse Show, Salem.

JULY
Chincoteague Pony Swim and Auction, Chincoteague Island.
Shakespeare Festival, Williamsburg.
Shenandoah Valley Music Fest, Orkney.

Great American Vintage Car Race, Norfolk.
Commonwealth Games, Roanoke.

AUGUST
East Coast Surfing Championships, Virginia Beach.
Old Fiddlers' Convention, Galax.
Hall of Fame Jousting Tournament (also June), Mount Solon.
Highlands Arts and Crafts Festival, Abingdon.

SEPTEMBER
State Fair, Richmond.
Foxfield Races, Charlottesville.
Great Peanut Bike Ride, Emporia.
Storytelling Festival, Tazewell.

OCTOBER
Virginia Craft and Folk Art Festival, Annadale.
Harvest Jubilee and World Tobacco Auctioneering Championship, Danville.
Railway Festival, Roanoke.
Steeplechase Gold Cup (also May), The Plains.
Annual North-South Skirmish, Winchester.

NOVEMBER
Waterfowl Week, Chincoteague.
Oyster Festival, Urbanna.

DECEMBER
Holiday Tours, Chatham, Danville, Fredericksburg, Jamestown, Virginia Beach, Warrenton, Williamsburg, Yorktown.

NOT TO BE MISSED

An eclectic selection of Virginia attractions

• **Observe spectacular showings of migratory birds** throughout the year at Assateague Island, including snow geese, swans, hawks, ducks, egrets, herons, plovers, and more.

• **Trace the legacy of Old Salts** from the Old and New World at the Mariners' Museum in Newport News. A plethora of artifacts and display present the history and lore of seafaring through the centuries.

• **Hoof it on horseback** over the mountainous back country of the Virginia Highlands Horse Trail at Mount Rogers or the scenic trails of Shenandoah National Park.

• **Take a driving tour** of the great plantation homes of the Tidewater country, along State Highway 5 from Williamsburg to Richmond. See the stately ancestral homes (some open to the public) of "first families" like Byrd, Harrison, Tyler, and Carter; also visit the nearby historic churches where they worshiped.

• **Treat yourself to a delectable taste of history** in Norfolk with an ice cream cone (using original 1905 equipment) from Doumar's famous drive-in, whose patriarch is credited with the wafer cone's concoction.

• **Stand in the footsteps of Patrick Henry** in Richmond's Saint John Church, where the patriot made his immortal declaration to the Virginia Convention in 1775. During summer months, watch a reenactment of this famous moment in American history.

• **Stage an evening's outdoor entertainment** at the popular Barter Theatre, the nation's first state-supported theatre, in Abingdon (regular currency now accepted in lieu of barter).

• **Visit the capital of the Confederacy** at Richmond. Tour the Old Hall of the state capitol, where Robert E. Lee was commissioned by the Confederate States of America and the Confederate congress met for three years. Stroll Capitol Square, with memorials to Confederate leaders, then proceed to the nearby Museum of the Confederacy at the Confederate White House.

• **Mix the miracles of nature with the kitsch of man** during trips to Luray Caverns in the Shenandoah Valley and the Natural Bridge Cavern near Lexington. Give equal time to the souvenir shops and attractions—including a wax museum with Adam and Eve and the Seven Days of Creation light show.

• **Board an old logging train** in Cass for a ride on the top of Bald Knob in the Allegheny Mountains. Watch the glimpses of wildlife (wildcats and even bears) on your way. Explore the quaint railroad museum for artifacts of the bygone era.

• **Traverse the pivotal theaters of the War Between the States** at Fredericksburg and Spotsylvania National Military parks, the sites of four major battles (and the mortal wounding of General "Stonewall" Jackson) and at Petersburg National Battlefield Park, where the ten-month-long conflict eventually yielded the defense of Richmond (and the Confederacy) to the Union.

• **Have your own pheasant under glass** after a day's hunt for Iranian black-necked pheasant or Japanese green pheasant in the Tidewater environs.

[For the full lowdown on Virginia, contact: Virginia Division of Tourism, 101 North Ninth Street, Richmond. 23219; 800/248-4833.]

VIRGINIA CLOSE-UP: *The annual pony penning at Chincoteague*

It's the stuff that storybooks are made of: the annual roundup and auction of the wild ponies of Assateague Island. Whether they are descendants of survivors of a shipwrecked Spanish galleon or of prolific herds interred by out-numbered colonists is of folkloric dispute, but they're doubtless the star attraction of a well-attended ritual of over sixty years. Come late July, members of the Chincoteague Volunteer Fire Company become volunteer cowboys, rounding up ponies on the southern end of the island and herding them across a narrow channel for a low-tide swim to Chincoteague. Next day, foals are auctioned to help support the fire company and control herd size. Afterwards unsold ponies swim back to the shores of Assateague. Before you go, read a charming chronicle of the event, *Misty of Chincoteague.*

Annual Wild Pony Roundup, Chincoteague Island

Ann Barrett Batson, a tenth-generation Southerner, was born in the piney woods of Mississippi and raised in Mobile, Alabama. Graduated from the University of Alabama, she has held positions in marketing and advertising management for the Coca-Cola Company, Danskin, and Ogilvy & Mather. She resides in Atlanta, where she has recently finished a novel.